Missouri Nature Viewing Guide

Your guide to 101 spectacular wildlife and nature viewing areas

Missouri Department of Conservation

Introduction

Again and again, Missourians have let us know that enjoying nature and watching wildlife are some of their favorite activities. This guide is intended to make those pursuits with binoculars and field guides a little easier.

We've asked the wildlife experts and naturalists of the state to help select Missouri's premier locations for outdoor experiences. Whether you enjoy nature from the trail, canoe, by cross-country or even from the car, you're sure to be pleased with the areas they've compiled.

We're committed to bringing more watchable wildlife and nature viewing opportunities to you. In the next few years, watch for improvements on areas across the state designed to help visitors experience and learn more about wildlife. As you travel through Missouri and the United States, watch for the binoculars signs to locate wildlife viewing sites. Follow the brown and white signs to find prime nature viewing areas and outdoor adventure.

Acknowledgements

Many agencies cooperated to bring you this guide and to make areas more accessible for enjoying nature. The City of Gladstone, Defenders of Wildlife, Ellisville Parks and Recreation, Jackson County Parks and Recreation, Mark Twain National Forest-USDA Forest Service, Martha Lafite Thompson Nature Sanctuary, Missouri Department of Natural Resources, National Park Service, St. Louis County Parks, University of Missouri, U.S. Army Corps of Engineers and U.S. Fish and Wildlife Service all have joined forces with the Missouri Department of Conservation to make this guide possible.

Contributions to site selection and review were made by outdoor enthusiasts and natural resource managers across Missouri – those who know the wild resources best. To all of them, we say thank you. Of special importance are the Missouri Department of Conservation's Nature Viewing Guide Committee members who gave hours of thoughtful selection and review to the sites:

George Buckner	George Hartman	Jim Johnson
Ed Keyser	Don Kurz	Kathy Love
Marlyn Miller	Rick Thom	

Book compilation staff:

editors
Martha Daniels, Charlotte Overby

contributors
Martha Daniels
Teresa Kight
John Bailey
Chris Dietrich
Wendy Gibbons
Amy Wieberg

photographer and photo editor
Jim Rathert

designer
Regina Troyer

cover photo
Glenn Chambers

Contents

Using the Guide

Whether you're an experienced wildlife watcher or a novice, this guide is designed to help you plan outdoor adventures. All listed sites are grouped into eight natural landscape regions of the state. Locate your general region of travel on the state map below, then refer to the regional map for specific sites within your traveling range.

Sites are listed numerically within each region and include a general description and featured wildlife, plants and habitats. Each site also has up to four wildlife symbols. These symbols are for quick reference and indicate wildlife you can expect to see. You'll find some locations reliable for viewing wildlife, while others may offer more of a challenge. Wilderness, rural and urban locations all have been included. Experiencing nature is thrilling, unpredictable and sometimes frustrating, so don't give up easily.

Site descriptions include habitats, as well as when and where some species are best viewed. Only typical or unusual species for the sites are listed, so those mentioned are just a hint of what you may see. Read about each site to learn of hiking trails or other special features. Symbols for recreational activities and facilities such as restrooms and picnic areas also are included for every site. Road directions accompany each site description.

Many sites are specially designated Missouri Natural Areas. Natural areas are biological communities or geological sites preserved and managed to perpetuate the natural character, diversity and ecological processes of Missouri's native landscapes.

Ownership of a site is listed by agency or organization, along with a phone number of the managing agency. At most sites, binocular logo signs should direct you to a point where your viewing experience can begin.

State Map

To help you experience nature in Missouri, we've divided the state into eight regions according to the natural divisions of the landscape. The 101 viewing sites are numbered consecutively region by region. Each region is described separately in this book. Directions are listed along with each site description. You can travel to most areas with the added help of a state highway map.

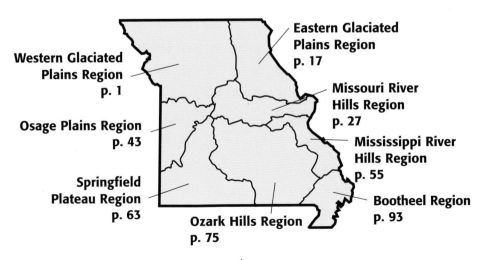

Western Glaciated Plains Region p. 1

Eastern Glaciated Plains Region p. 17

Osage Plains Region p. 43

Missouri River Hills Region p. 27

Mississippi River Hills Region p. 55

Springfield Plateau Region p. 63

Bootheel Region p. 93

Ozark Hills Region p. 75

Symbols for Viewing Opportunities and Facilities

Nature symbols •

 Songbirds

 Upland birds

 Waterfowl

 Wading birds

 Shorebirds

 Birds of prey

 Small mammals

 Hoofed mammals

 Carnivores

 Freshwater mammals

 Bats

 Fish

 Reptiles/ amphibians

 Wildflowers/ trees

 Insects

Facility symbols •

 Parking

 Restrooms

 Picnic areas

 Hiking trail

 Disabled accessible

 Small boats

 Large boats

 Food service

 Boat ramps

 Primitive camping

 Camping facilities

 Lodging

 Visitor center

 Interpretive trail

 Auto tour

Etiquette in the Outdoors

Wild animals and plants easily are disturbed by too much human activity. Viewing disturbance may cause an animal to leave the area or abandon a nest or den.

Keep a safe distance. If an animal stops feeding or stands up from resting, you may be disrupting its routine. Wild animals need to go about their daily matters undisturbed. Because of you, wildlife may waste energy searching for other sources of food or leave an area that was safe from predators.

Approaching wildlife too closely, especially white-tailed deer, black bear or other large animals, is dangerous. If an animal looks sick or acts strangely, stay clear.

Remember to watch for wildlife all around you, not just on the ground. Gray treefrogs, for example, have "sticky" toe pads that enable them to hide on vertical surfaces, such as rough tree bark or leaves.

Avoid disturbing the young and their nests. Baby animals look irresistible, but are best left in the wild. They only appear to be orphaned or abandoned. Chances are, a parent is nearby watching you and waiting to care for the young. Do not touch or handle young wildlife.

Follow signs and obey posted rules. Rules prohibiting removing, touching and feeding wildlife are extremely important. When humans feed animals, the animals' chances for survival may be jeopardized. Animals fed by humans tend to lose their sense of place in the natural world and may grow dependent on handouts or become hostile toward humans. In addition, pets are best left at home or in your vehicle while you're watching wildlife. Dogs or other pets may chase or injure wildlife, so keep your pets secure and away from restricted areas.

Be courteous to others. Entering an area and disturbing visitors, animals and plants by making noise, sudden motions or moving off designated trails can destroy the resource. Be polite and share a positive experience with others. Take special care not to damage the habitat as you hike; pack out all litter and leave the area better than you found it. Litter and disturbance can restrict future use of the area by humans and wildlife.

Respect the rights of private landowners. Always gain permission before entering or crossing private property.

Stay within the law. Be sure to leave feathers, eggs, nests or animals where you find them and do not pull or dig plants. Removing pieces of nature can be harmful to the resource, and, in most cases, is against the law.

Viewing Hints

When you head for the woods and fields in search of wildlife, remember that the animals and plants you hope to see may not always be easy to find. Here are some ways to increase your chances of viewing wildlife in natural settings.

Choose the right place. If you're looking for a specific plant or animal, learn the preferred habitat of the species. Animals live only where they'll find the right food, water and shelter. Water attracts wildlife of all kinds. Some of the best viewing areas are along rivers, streams, marshes or near ponds and lakes.

Pick the right time. The first and last hours of daylight are best for viewing wildlife. Avoid looking for mammals and birds in the heat of a summer day. However, most amphibians, reptiles and insects can best be observed as temperatures rise in the summer. Keep in mind that many public areas are open to hunting and fishing. Check area regulations and take proper precautions (such as wearing blaze orange) during popular seasons.

Identify appropriate seasons of the year. Some animals, such as waterfowl and bald eagles, are best seen at specific times of migration and are more dependable for viewing than coyotes or salamanders. Warblers and other songbirds are travelers too, and the most species are seen in spring and fall. Plants are very seasonal; most wildflowers and trees bloom for only a short period, depending on weather conditions.

Watch for telltale signs. Tracks in mud, gnawed saplings, nests, freshly dug soil, a den or trampled leaves are all clues to the wildlife using an area. Plan to spend some time observing habitats and finding the signs, in addition to viewing the wildlife.

Be still, quiet and patient. Move slowly to get in place for viewing. Loud noise and quick movements disturb and alarm wildlife. Sometimes staying in your car or boat is the best cover to take; some wildlife are used to seeing vehicles nearby and will continue undisturbed so you can watch. Make use of other available cover, such as a shrub, viewing blind or observation platform. When cover isn't nearby, sit quietly. Allow time for the animals to enter or return to a feeding or travel area.

Use binoculars. For a close-up look and to observe an animal's activity, use binoculars, a spotting scope or camera with a telephoto lens. Be careful not to get too close to the animal. If the animal acts alarmed, stops feeding or becomes nervous, move away slowly or sit quietly until it resumes normal behavior.

Consult experts, maps and books. Visit with naturalists or other conservationists before planning your trip. They can help you locate areas appropriate for the season. Attend programs offered at local nature centers. Share your experiences with people you meet. Take along field guides, and remember to check the weather forecast to make sure conditions will allow safe access to the area you'll be visiting.

Take the memory home. This guide is designed to help you enjoy and experience the Missouri outdoors. Keep a diary as a reminder of the exceptional viewing you've experienced. In your pursuits, we hope you find pleasure in our state's beautiful resources – a feeling that becomes a commitment to protecting Missouri's natural integrity for you and generations to come.

Missouri Habitats

Missouri's landscape has a wealth of grasslands and forested hills, clear streams and big rivers. There are six basic habitat types described here to help you recognize the plants and animals you're likely to encounter.

Grassland – A rolling landscape of grasses once covered a third of the state, now reduced to tallgrass prairie remnants scattered across the Western Glaciated Plains and the Osage Plains. The glades and savannas of southern Missouri also are grasslands with prairie wildflowers and animals.

Forest – Missouri's forest land originally covered much of eastern and southern Missouri, and this land is a mixture of hardwood trees commonly called "oak-hickory forest." Portions of the Ozark Hills also are home to the state's only native pine, shortleaf pine, which grows in forests mixed with oaks.

River bottomland – The Mississippi, Missouri and many other rivers and large streams flood the broad flat land outside their banks. Hardwood trees commonly are found in these river bottomlands, but so are prairies, backwater marshes and swamps.

Rivers and streams – From clear, spring-fed Ozark streams to the great, muddy Missouri and Mississippi rivers, Missouri has one of the most diverse collections of rivers and streams in the United States. Many beautiful and unusual animals inhabit these waterways, and wildlife of all kinds are attracted to the riparian zone bordering these habitats.

Wetlands – Before European settlement, chains of wetlands bounded the rivers of northern Missouri while swamps were abundant in the Bootheel. A few of these wetlands are now key lands for migrating waterfowl to stop and feed in spring and fall. Pockets of moist soil known as seeps and fens are found throughout the state, and are associated with both prairies and forests.

Caves, springs and sinkholes – Karst features and caves occur throughout southern Missouri. Caves are fragile environments containing animals adapted to life in complete darkness. Sinkholes funnel water down to underground streams that pour out at surface springs and cave openings.

Western Glaciated Plains

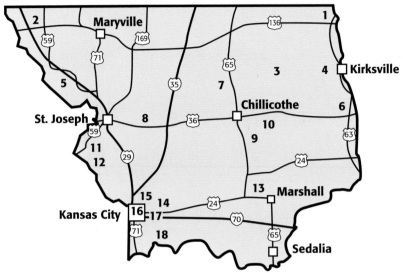

1 Rebel's Cove Conservation Area
2 Star School Hill Prairie Conservation Area
3 Locust Creek Conservation Area
4 Big Creek Conservation Area and Thousand Hills State Park
5 Squaw Creek National Wildlife Refuge
6 Atlanta Conservation Area, Long Branch Lake and Long Branch State Park
7 Poosey Conservation Area
8 Pony Express Lake Conservation Area
9 Fountain Grove Conservation Area and Swan Lake National Wildlife Refuge
10 Pershing State Park
11 Bluffwoods Conservation Area
12 Little Bean Marsh Conservation Area
13 Grand Pass Conservation Area
14 Cooley Lake Conservation Area
15 Martha Lafite Thompson Nature Sanctuary
16 Maple Woods Natural Area
17 Burr Oak Woods Conservation Area and Nature Center
18 Fleming Park

During the ice age, glaciers moved across these plains and left silt, sand, gravel and boulders in their paths. Strong winds then drifted the fine dust particles into deep loess soils. Loess soils are loose and silty, piled high by wind erosion.

Before European settlement, more than half this region's hills and ridges were tallgrass prairie. Today, the prairie has almost disappeared, converted into some of the most fertile agricultural land in the world.

Forests wound along the slow, muddy streams and rivers. The Missouri River once was wide and shallow as it flowed through this region. Many islands, sloughs and backwaters attracted a wealth of wildlife. The rivers, too, have been changed, but the wetland areas that remain along their courses offer some of the best wildlife viewing opportunities in Missouri.

Though not as accomplished as beaver at building homes, muskrat build smaller versions out of similar materials, such as cattails and other aquatic plants stems.

1 Rebel's Cove Conservation Area

Rebel's Cove has some outstanding wetland habitat, as well as a natural stretch of north Missouri river. The winding channel of the Chariton River has created many oxbow lakes and marshes, which are prime areas for watching shorebirds, wading birds and waterfowl. At a heronry on the area, you can see great blue herons.

Marshes on Rebel's Cove attract ducks, Canada geese, songbirds, muskrat, beaver and river otters. Watch for ring-necked pheasant, bobwhite quail, wild turkeys, red-tailed hawks, owls and white-tailed deer in the grasslands. Mature forests provide serene areas to enjoy trees and woodland wildflowers.

Size: 4,176 acres   **Nearest town:** Kirksville

Location: From Kirksville, travel north on U.S. 63 for 19 miles to Highway 136. On 136, turn west, and travel 8 miles to Highway N. Take N north 5.1 miles to the area entrance on the right. Continue on the gravel road to parking areas and the river access. A natural marsh can be reached by continuing north on N for 1.3 miles and turning right on the gravel road.

Contact: Missouri Department of Conservation, 2500 S. Halliburton, Kirksville, MO 63501, (816) 785-2420

2 Star School Hill Prairie Conservation Area

Star School Hill Prairie is in a region of rugged loess river hills, once covered by tallgrass prairie. "Loess" refers to the type of soil – a loose soil of silt deposited by wind erosion. At Star School Hill Prairie you'll find many prairie plants that are rare in Missouri, but more common to the western Great Plains: yucca, downy painted cup, blazing star and skeleton plant.

On the conservation area – part of which is a Designated Natural Area – you're likely to see white-tailed deer, bobwhite quail, cottontail rabbit and wild turkey. Watch for songbirds and birds of prey, especially great-horned owls and red-tailed hawks. Climb to the hilltops for a scenic view of the Missouri River Valley below.

Size: 129 acres   **Nearest town:** Rock Port

Location: From the junction of Highway 275 and 136 north of Rock Port, take 275 north for 14 miles to the area entrance on the right side of the highway.

Contact: Missouri Department of Conservation, 701 NE College, St. Joseph, MO 64507, (816) 271-3100

Penstemon grandiflorus, or beard-tongue, is endangered.

3 Locust Creek Conservation Area

A stretch of Locust Creek's flood plain, surrounded by woodlands and open fields, provides scenic north Missouri wildlife viewing. Visit the forests to see warblers during spring migration. Watch for barred owls, wild turkeys and white-tailed deer near woods at dawn and dusk. Great blue herons, green herons, beaver and muskrat are attracted to the wetlands and shallows along Locust Creek. A few short field trails provide access to the creek and ponds, but you'll find some of the best wildlife viewing by hiking cross-country.

Size: 3,162 acres   **Nearest town:** Milan

Location: From the junction of Highway 5 and Highway E in Milan, travel west on E for 4 miles to a gravel road. Turn south on the gravel road for 1 mile to the parking area.

Contact: Missouri Department of Conservation, 2500 S. Halliburton, Kirksville, MO 63501, (816) 785-2420

4 Big Creek Conservation Area and Thousand Hills State Park

Rocky hills, wooded ravines and grassy ridges at Big Creek Conservation Area and Thousand Hills State Park are habitat for white-tailed deer, cottontail rabbits, red fox, squirrels, wild turkeys and songbirds. Thousand Hills Trail travels 5 miles along a high ridge through several habitat types, offering a spectacular view of the surrounding hills and lake. A grove of large-toothed aspen, a rare Missouri tree, also is found near the trail.

Beaver can be seen year 'round along Big Creek and Forest Lake. Groups of turkey vultures roost on the area in late summer and fall, so watch for hundreds of them soaring above the lake in the evening. To enjoy spring woodland wildflowers and songbirds, hike one of the three shorter trails at Thousand Hills State Park.

Big Creek Conservation Area

Size: 1,201 acres   **Nearest town:** Kirksville

Location: Travel south from Kirksville on U.S. 63 for 2 miles to Highway 11. Take 11 west for 1.6 miles to County Road H. Travel north on H for 1.6 miles to the first gravel road on the left (CR 226), and follow the road to the Thousand Hills Trailhead parking lot.

Contact: Missouri Department of Conservation, 2500 S. Halliburton, Kirksville, MO 63501, (816) 785-2420

Thousand Hills State Park

Size: 3,215 acres   **Nearest town:** Kirksville

Location: Travel on U.S. 63 north of Kirksville for .5 mile to Highway 6. Turn west on Highway 6 for 3 miles to Highway 157. Travel south on 157 to the park entrance.

Contact: Missouri Department of Natural Resources, Thousand Hills State Park, Route 3, Kirksville, MO 63501, (800) 334-6946

Mallards often winter in Missouri and are among the most common and earliest spring migrants. They frequent shallow marsh and flooded timber areas.

5 Squaw Creek National Wildlife Refuge

Several hundred thousand snow geese and ducks arrive here each year – an incredible scene as the sky fills with a winding mass of waterfowl at dusk and dawn. Snow geese, white pelicans and other waterfowl stop at Squaw Creek to group and feed during migration.

Hundreds of bald eagles also winter at the refuge, feeding on injured waterfowl. Squaw Creek attracts a larger concentration of eagles than any other wintering site in the state. The auto tour road that circles the marsh and pools provides excellent wildlife viewing from your car, especially in fall and winter when white-tailed deer, coyotes and other wildlife are active at dusk. Be sure to watch the marsh and surrounding waterways for beaver and muskrat.

Loess Bluff Trail at the refuge headquarters and the bluff trail at Jamerson C. McCormack Loess Mounds Natural Area (2 miles to the south) take you up high bluffs for a scenic view of the Missouri River and the refuge's large basin of water. For additional wildlife viewing and recreation, visit nearby Big Lake State Park.

Size: 7,200 acres   **Nearest town:** Mound City

Location: From Mound City, take Interstate 29 south 5 miles to U.S. 159. Travel west on 159 for 2.3 miles to the refuge entrance and visitor center.

Contact: Squaw Creek National Wildlife Refuge, P.O. Box 101, Mound City, MO 64470, (816) 442-3187

6 Atlanta Conservation Area, Long Branch Lake and Long Branch State Park

Gently rolling woodlands and fields along the north edge of Long Branch Lake are habitat for both woodland and wetland wildlife. During spring and fall migrations, ducks, geese, sandpipers and plovers stop at the lake. The East Fork of Little Chariton River and Long Branch Creek support marshy areas for egrets and herons to wade and fish. Watch for white-tailed deer, wild turkey and bobwhite quail where the woods meet the fields. Hiking old roads on the area takes you over hills and past several wetlands and streams.

For more wildlife viewing nearby, visit Long Branch Lake and Long Branch State Park to the south of the conservation area. Look for beaver and signs of their work around the lake shore. At the lake and state park you'll find trails through forest, savanna and restored prairie. Stop, too, at the U.S. Army Corps of Engineers visitor center and overlook on the east side of the dam for information on seasonal wildlife.

Great egrets are among the most graceful and showy of all wading birds. They feed on frogs, snakes and fish in wetlands.

Size: 4,474 acres

Nearest town: Macon

Locations: Atlanta Conservation Area – from Macon, travel 12 miles north on U.S. 63 to County Road J. Turn west, and go 2 miles to County Road RA. Turn south, and follow RA for 3 miles to the parking area. Long Branch Lake and State Park – from Macon, travel west on U.S. 36 for 2 miles.

Contact for Atlanta Conservation Area: Missouri Department of Conservation, 2500 S. Halliburton, Kirksville, MO 63501, (816) 785-2420

Contact for Long Branch Lake: U.S. Army Corps of Engineers, Long Branch Project Office, Route 4, Box 6, Macon, MO 63552, (816)385-2108

Contact for Long Branch State Park: Missouri Department of Natural Resources, Long Branch State Park, 28615 Visitor Center Road, Macon, MO 63552, (800) 334-6946

7 Poosey Conservation Area

A mix of grasslands and hardwood forests covers Poosey Conservation Area. You're most likely to see white-tailed deer, red fox, raccoons, squirrels, wild turkeys and bobwhite quail while visiting the area. There are many species of grassland songbirds, including Henslow's and grasshopper sparrows, and several woodland warblers.

Visit the 192-acre Indian Creek Community Lake at dawn and dusk to see deer, waterfowl and wading birds. While you're visiting the area in spring, watch for charred grasses and other signs of past fires. Controlled fires are used here to promote wildlife diversity and to maintain remnant prairies.

Size: 4,604 acres   **Nearest town:** Chillicothe

Location: From Chillicothe, travel north on U.S. 65 for 1 mile to Highway 190. Turn west on 190, and go 6 miles to County Road A. Turn north on A, and drive 8.5 miles to the parking area on the south side of the road.

Contact: Missouri Department of Conservation, Route 1, Box 122B, Chillicothe, MO 64601, (816) 646-6122

8 Pony Express Lake Conservation Area

Pony Express Lake Conservation Area's grasslands rise above wooded valleys. A marsh, lakes and more than 30 ponds are all good locations for viewing wildlife. These sites attract Canada geese, ducks, wading birds and shorebirds, along with several species of frogs and turtles. Enjoy the prairie and wetland wildlife as you drive down area roadways, or hike the trail for viewing opportunities.

From May through August, showy prairie wildflowers bloom in the grasslands located in the southwest corner. Watch for songbirds, wild turkeys, white-tailed deer, bobwhite quail and cottontail rabbits feeding in the prairie grasses and wooded draws. Seasonal changes are worth experiencing at Pony Express, so visit throughout the year.

Size: 3,150 acres   **Nearest town:** St. Joseph

Location: Travel east 30 miles from St. Joseph on U.S. 36 to Highway 33. Turn north on 33, and drive 2 miles to Highway RA. Follow RA west 1.3 miles to the area entrance.

Contact: Missouri Department of Conservation, 701 NE College, St. Joseph, MO 64507, (816) 271-3100

9 Fountain Grove Conservation Area and Swan Lake National Wildlife Refuge

Fountain Grove and Swan Lake are extensive wetlands – prime areas to watch waterfowl, shorebirds, bald eagles and aquatic mammals. During spring and summer at Fountain Grove, watch for warblers and herons traveling along the Grand River. Fall and winter bring thousands of snow and Canada geese to both areas for a stop during migration.

February, March, October and November are the best months to see shoveler, pintail, widgeon, teal, ring-necked ducks and cormorants. Bald eagles perch in large trees around open water to feed on injured waterfowl, and northern harriers and ospreys hunt here. As many as 1,500 white pelicans stop at both areas in spring and fall.

While you're traveling the areas, watch for river otters and beaver swimming in the pools and lakes, and coyotes moving across the fields. Swan Lake has an observation tower, visitor center and auto tour, and at both areas, follow the levees, service roads and trails for the best wildlife viewing. Note that waterfowl refuge areas are restricted to the public from October 15 until waterfowl season closes in mid-February. Call ahead to check for the specific date.

The Missouri Department of Conservation conducts an annual eagle count. Since 1976, the number of eagles in Missouri has tripled. The winter population now is about 2,200.

Feathers of birds in the cormorant family, such as this double-crested cormorant, are not waterproof. They become so water-sodden after fishing underwater, that the bird must hold its wings open in the breeze and sun to dry.

Fountain Grove Conservation Area

Size: 7,154 acres   **Nearest town:** Chillicothe

Location: Travel east from Chillicothe on U.S. 36 for 12 miles to Meadville. Turn south on County Road W, and drive 5 miles to the area entrance and headquarters.

Contact: Missouri Department of Conservation, Route 1, Box 122B, Chillicothe, MO 64601, (816) 646-6122

Swan Lake National Wildlife Refuge

Size: 10,670 acres   **Nearest town:** Chillicothe

Location: Travel east from Chillicothe on U.S. 36 for 19 miles to Highway 139. Take 139 south 12 miles to Sumner. Follow County Road RA south to the refuge entrance.

Contact: Swan Lake National Wildlife Refuge, P.O. Box 68, Sumner, MO 64681, (816) 856-3323

10 Pershing State Park

A trip to Pershing State Park gives you a glimpse of northern Missouri as it was before settlement. A boardwalk trail leads to an observation platform overlooking a 1,000-acre wet prairie. You'll find the prairie sprinkled with color in spring and summer as water smartweed, pale green orchid, swamp milkweed and tickseed sunflower bloom. Locust Creek Natural Area is a wet bottomland forest with large cottonwoods, river birch, and bur, pin and swamp white oaks. Clumps of ostrich ferns are scattered throughout the forest understory.

Marshes and oxbow lakes created by Locust Creek attract bald eagles in winter and barred owls throughout the year. Watch for belted kingfishers and blue-winged teal along the creek. This stretch of Locust Creek is a rich, winding river system – a rare habitat of the Western Glaciated Plains.

Size: 2,909 acres   **Nearest town:** Brookfield

Location: Take U.S. 36 west 7 miles from Brookfield to Highway 130. Travel south on 130 for 1 mile to the park entrance.

Contact: Missouri Department of Natural Resources, Pershing State Park, Laclede, MO 64651, (800) 334-6946

11 Bluffwoods Conservation Area

Bluffwoods is a remnant of the lush forests that once grew along the bluffs above the Missouri River. Watch for woodland wildflowers, migratory songbirds, raccoon, white-tailed deer, red and gray fox, cottontail rabbit and opossum in the deep woods and open ridges. Be on the lookout for ruffed grouse in the forested areas. At the picnic area located at the southwest end of Bluffwoods, you'll find the trailhead for Lone Pine Trail – a climb through the woods to open ridge tops and a spectacular view of the Missouri River Valley.

Size: 2,344 acres   **Nearest town:** St. Joseph

Location: From St. Joseph, travel south 8 miles on U.S. 59 to County Road 219. Look for signs leading to the area on the east side of the highway.

Contact: Missouri Department of Conservation, 701 NE College, St. Joseph, MO 64507, (816) 271-3100

Prothonotary warblers are the only warblers in the eastern United States that nest in tree cavities.

12 Little Bean Marsh Conservation Area

Noted in the journals of Lewis and Clark for hosting an abundance of wildlife, Little Bean Marsh has a history of being a wildlife watcher's haven. It is a small marsh along the Missouri River where prothonotary warblers, marsh wrens, bitterns, rails and herons can be seen in sloughs and backwaters from spring through summer. Sedges, rushes, lotus and bladderwort (a small carnivorous plant) are among the marsh's plant life.

A viewing tower located a short distance from the parking lot provides a panoramic view of the marsh, and the tower also is a good place for viewing the waterfowl, bald eagles and marsh hawks of winter. A portion of Little Bean Marsh is a Designated Natural Area.

Size: 427 acres   **Nearest town:** St. Joseph

Location: From St. Joseph, take U.S. 59 south 18 miles to Highway 45. Continue south 4 miles on Highway 45 to the area entrance on the right. The road takes you along the edge of Bean Lake to the parking area.

Contact: Missouri Department of Conservation, 701 NE College, St. Joseph, MO 64507, (816) 271-3100

Identifying snow geese can be tricky. Some are white with black wing tips. Others are bluish gray with white heads. They nest in mixed colonies, color forms intermingled.

13 Grand Pass Conservation Area

Grand Pass is recognized as a waterfowl area, but expect to see many migratory wading birds and shorebirds, in addition to geese and ducks. Habitats on the area include forest, wetland, river island and field. In the bottomland forest, you'll see migratory songbirds and nesting wood ducks. Canada and snow geese come to the wetlands in winter, and shorebirds feed along the river islands and mudflats in spring. Levees, roads and trails at Grand Pass are excellent for bird viewing, especially in February and March.

Size: 4,711 acres **Nearest town:** Marshall

Location: From Marshall, travel northwest 7 miles on U.S. 65 to County Road N. Turn north on N for 5.5 miles to the area headquarters on the west side of the road.

Contact: Missouri Department of Conservation, 1014 Thompson Blvd., Sedalia MO 65301, (816) 530-5500

While most herons are flying to their roosts for the night, black-crowned night herons scatter over the marshes to feed, avoiding competition.

14 Cooley Lake Conservation Area

As one of the few remaining oxbow lakes in northwest Missouri, Cooley Lake is a gathering spot for shorebirds, waterfowl and wading birds migrating along the Missouri River. The area is close to Kansas City and attracts egrets, bitterns, black-crowned night herons, green herons, great blue herons and mallard and wood ducks. The best viewing seasons are during fall and spring migrations, but birds also nest and feed along the lake year 'round. The site is a waterfowl refuge and is closed October 15 to mid-January. A special viewing day is offered in fall.

Size: 917 acres   **Nearest town:** Liberty

Location: From Liberty, take Highway 210 east 9 miles to the area entrance on the north side of the road.

Contact: Missouri Department of Conservation, 701 NE College, St. Joseph, MO 64507, (816) 271-3100

15 Martha Lafite Thompson Nature Sanctuary

This private nature sanctuary may be small, but it has several habitats and abundant wildlife. On Woodland Trail, you travel through an oak-hickory forest among woodland wildflowers. In spring, the songs of nesting tanagers, wood thrushes and chuck-will's-widows blend with chorusing frogs of a small pond.

Rush Creek Trail takes you along a beautiful stream with kingfishers, wood ducks, migrating warblers and raccoons. Summer and fall bring colorful wildflowers and butterflies to Prairie Trail. South Meadow Trail winds through upland meadows, good places for observing cottontail rabbits, white-tailed deer and woodpeckers. Visit the nature center in winter to view songbirds at feeder stations. For additional nature study, visit nearby Rush Creek Conservation Area.

Size: 100 acres   **Nearest town:** Liberty

Location: From Interstate 35 in Liberty, take Highway 152 (Kansas Street) east 2 miles to Jewell Street. Turn south on Jewell, and go 2 blocks to Richfield Road. Take Richfield west across a wooden railroad bridge, continue .5 block to LaFrenz Road, and turn north to the nature sanctuary entrance.

Contact: Martha Lafite Thompson Nature Sanctuary, 407 N. LaFrenz Rd., Liberty, MO 64068, (816) 781-8598

16 Maple Woods Natural Area

Maple Woods is a stately forest located just a few miles north of downtown Kansas City. The site is tranquil, and a dense tree canopy shades the understory in summer. An 18-acre natural area of old-growth forest has many spring wildflowers and beautiful fall colors from sugar maple, red oak, white oak and basswood trees. Hiking trails take you to the natural area where songbirds, cottontail rabbit, squirrel, white-tailed deer, red fox and woodland wildflowers are found.

Size: 39 acres   **Nearest town:** Kansas City

Location: Travel north on Interstate 29 across the Missouri River 5.5 miles to U.S. 169. Go north on 169 for 4.5 miles to Highway 152 (Barry Road). Turn east on 152, and drive .8 mile to North Oak. Turn south on North Oak for 1.1 miles to NE 76th Street. Turn east on NE 76th Street, and continue 1.5 miles.

Contact: City of Gladstone, 7010 N. Holmes, Gladstone, MO 64118, (816) 436-2200

Bethany Falls Trail is considered by hiking enthusiasts to be one of the Kansas City area's best trails. It is located at the Burr Oak Woods Conservation Nature Center – one of four nature centers operated by the Missouri Department of Conservation.

17 Burr Oak Woods Conservation Area and Nature Center

Only a short distance from Kansas City, Burr Oak Woods has three trails that take you through the area's hardwood forests, tallgrass prairie planting and glade. Watch for wild turkey, white-tailed deer, raccoon, cottontail rabbit and opossum while hiking the trails. Bethany Falls Trail is a 1.3-mile trail which loops through a 33-acre natural area. The trail takes you across a prairie stream and through a natural maze of Bethany Falls limestone outcrops and boulders.

Two other trails on the area – the 1.5-mile Wildlife Habitat Trail and the .5-mile paved Discovery Trail – pass through oak-hickory and bottomland forests, old fields and other habitats. The nature center has indoor exhibits, and a bird feeding station and wildlife viewing area so you can watch American goldfinch, woodpecker, nuthatch and other songbirds.

Size: 1,071 acres   **Nearest town:** Blue Springs

Location: From Interstate 70 in Blue Springs, travel north 1.2 miles on Highway 7 to NW Park Road. Turn west on NW Park Road .3 mile to the front gate.

Contact: Burr Oak Woods Conservation Nature Center, Missouri Department of Conservation, 1401 NW Park Rd., Blue Springs, MO 64015, (816) 228-3766

18 Fleming Park

Fleming Park, which lies in a zone where the Osage Plains and Western Glaciated Plains natural divisions meet, has a mix of woods, open grasslands and old fields. A large stand of jack pines across from Shelter 14 is a good spot to see crossbills, kinglets and red-breasted nuthatches in winter, and warblers and tanagers in spring. Eagles and ospreys, as well as great horned, barred and screech owls, are some of the raptor species you'll see at Lake Jacomo and Blue Springs Lake.

In late winter, watch for red fox, white-tailed deer, wild turkey, an occasional bobcat and woodcock in the grasslands. Winter waterfowl viewing is a highlight at area lakes. Expect to see goldeneye, bufflehead, ringneck and canvasback ducks, and thousands of migrating Canada and snow geese. A few loons stop at the lakes each winter. You'll also find a visitor center and native wildlife exhibit at the park.

Size: 7,809 acres   **Nearest town:** Blue Springs

Location: From Interstate 70 in Blue Springs, take Highway 7 south 1.5 miles to U.S. 40. Travel west on 40 for 2 miles to Woods Chapel Road. Take Woods Chapel Road south 1 mile, and follow the signs to the lake entrance.

Contact: Jackson County Parks and Recreation, 22807 Woods Chapel Rd., Blue Springs, MO 64015, (816) 795-8200

The bufflehead is a member of the merganser and sea duck group of ducks, commonly called "divers." They arrive in Missouri by late February and continue to move through the state during March and early April.

Eastern Glaciated Plains

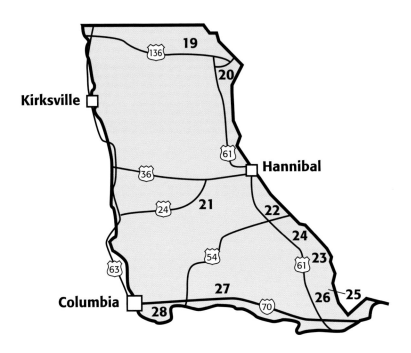

19 Fox Valley Lake Conservation Area
20 Rose Pond Conservation Area
21 Mark Twain Lake
22 Ted Shanks Conservation Area
23 Clarence Cannon National
Wildlife Refuge

24 Lock and Dam #24
25 Lock and Dam #25
26 Cuivre River State Park
27 Danville and Whetstone Creek
Conservation Areas
28 Tucker Prairie

In northeastern Missouri, glaciers leveled the land leaving plains similar to the grasslands of the West. Deciduous forests covered the hills along waterways, while rocky soils and tallgrass prairies stretched across the level uplands.

Today, much of the region's rich soils are used for agriculture. The southeastern part of the region, the Lincoln Hills, rises high above the Mississippi River. The abrupt hills contain steep cliffs, forests and rare glades, along with cave features common to the Ozark Hills. Amethyst shooting stars and pickerel frogs are a sampling of the many plants and animals that live here.

Moles often are characterized as hermits. They live in isolation except when mating. They are most active on damp, cloudy days.

19 Fox Valley Lake Conservation Area

The most exciting wildlife watching at Fox Valley is along a marsh and natural stretch of the Fox River. Rolling hills covered with hardwood forests and grasslands are home to warblers, white-tailed deer and wild turkeys. You'll find bobwhite quail, sparrows and coyotes feeding in open fields. Watch for short-eared owls in the white pine plantation. Nestled in the wooded hills is a 100-acre lake with many fingers and coves. Watch for great blue herons, ducks, muskrat, mink and beaver at the 15-acre marsh and shorebird area along the Fox River.

Size: 2,159 acres   **Nearest town:** Kahoka

Location: From the junction of highways 136 and 81 in Kahoka, travel north on 81 for 6.5 miles to County Road NN. Turn west on NN, and travel 2.8 miles to the area entrance.

Contact: Missouri Department of Conservation, 2500 S. Halliburton, Kirksville, MO 63501, (816) 785-2420

20 Rose Pond Conservation Area

At Rose Pond, deep sandy soils and a wetland with bulrush form a very rare Missouri landscape. Sand was deposited in the area by the Des Moines River many years ago. For the best bird viewing, walk the sandy lane east from the parking area. The road crosses the center of the marsh.

Late summer is the best time to see egrets and great blue and black-crowned night herons wading in the marsh north of the lane. If you're patient, you may see American and least bitterns, rails or gallinules feeding in the bulrushes. Watch for turtles basking on logs.

Size: 379 acres   **Nearest town:** Kahoka

Location: From Kahoka, take Highway 136 east 8 miles to Wayland, then south for 2 miles to U.S. 61. Take 61 northeast 5 miles to a gravel road on the south. Travel 2.5 miles south on the gravel road to the parking area on the left.

Contact: Missouri Department of Conservation, 2500 S. Halliburton, Kirksville, MO 63501, (816) 785-2420

Western painted turtles live in ponds, oxbow lakes, drainage ditches or slow-moving rivers, especially where there is plenty of mud on the bottom and aquatic vegetation. They are active from late March to October when the temperature is 68 degrees or above. They alternately bask on logs and forage for food during the day. At night, they sleep in pools or ponds.

21 Mark Twain Lake

Hiking trails, a waterfowl refuge and other areas around Mark Twain Lake provide waterfowl and songbird viewing, as well as scenic vistas. For example, hike the Ray Behrens Recreation Area's Hickory Bluff Trail for a scenic view of the lake and to see woodland wildflowers and songbirds. At the waterfowl refuge located along the Middle Fork Salt River, early morning is the best time to see ducks, geese and shorebirds. Waterfowl numbers peak from October 15 to December 15.

Turkey vultures soar in large groups above the lake in summer, and the M. W. Boudreaux Visitor Center is a good vantage point for vulture viewing. Venture out to the overlooks near the visitor center in late winter to watch bald eagles. (The center is closed December through March.)

Hike the 7.5-mile Lick Creek Trail to see rich woodlands with white-tailed deer and wild turkey, plus a carpet of wildflowers in spring and fall. Viewing from a vehicle is best at nearby Indian Creek Recreation Area, where you'll enjoy wildlife and landscapes of forest, prairie and lake coves.

Size: 55,000 acres   **Nearest town:** Hannibal

Location: From Hannibal, take U.S. 36 west 20 miles to County Road J. Turn south on J for 10 miles, cross Clarence Cannon Dam, and look for the M. W. Boudreaux Visitor Center on the west side of the road.

Contact: Mark Twain Lake Management Office, Route 2, Box 20A, Monroe City, MO 63456-9359, (314) 735-4097

To increase your chances of spotting a rabbit, use a stop-and-start approach to scare them up. They often sit tight and remain hidden in cover until you walk past.

Tucked between the Mississippi and Salt rivers, the Shanks area is a wetland teeming with waterfowl, songbirds, mammals and wildflowers. Seven river islands, a wetland complex, large bottomland forests and many waterfowl management pools make up the area. Prairie Slough and Oval Lake are designated natural areas within the Shanks area.

For the best bird viewing, visit the sloughs and marshes in spring and summer to see ducks, geese, prothonotary warblers, northern parulas, swamp sparrows and marsh wrens. Red-tailed hawks, northern harriers, peregrine falcons, marsh hawks and ospreys are among the wintering raptors you may see throughout the area.

Despite the length of its bill, the lesser yellowlegs does not probe for food. Rather, it uses the bill to snatch insects and small fish.

Hiking trails on the levees cross the marsh and wetlands at the junction of the rivers. Here, watch for American and least bitterns, sandpipers, egrets, green herons, black-crowned night herons, yellowlegs, snipes and king rails. Bald eagles, too, return each winter to hunt the waters of the Shanks area. Watch for other water wildlife, such as river otters, beaver, muskrat, mink and weasels. The levee trails are open in winter, spring and summer, but portions of the area are closed October 15 through early December for waterfowl season.

For a scenic view of the Mississippi River and conservation area, Highway and Transportation Department overlooks are located north of the Shanks area on Highway 79.

Size: 6,636 acres   **Nearest town:** Hannibal

Location: From Hannibal, travel south 19 miles on Highway 79 to County Road TT. Turn east on TT, and go 1 mile to the area entrance.

Contact: Ted Shanks Conservation Area, Missouri Department of Conservation, Box 13, Ashburn, MO 63433, (314) 754-6171

Blue-winged teal migrate from as far south as Peru and Brazil. Several thousand can be seen on most Missouri wetland areas from mid-March through much of April.

23 Clarence Cannon National Wildlife Refuge

Thousands of mallards, wood ducks, pintails, widgeons, teal, shovelers and Canada and snow geese stop at Clarence Cannon while migrating along the Mississippi flyway in spring and fall. Prime migration is October through November and March through April. The refuge is a travel stop where ducks and geese can find food and resting areas. In spring and summer, watch for nesting wood ducks, blue-winged teal, spotted sandpipers and herons.

Other birds to watch wading through the wetlands include great egrets, least bitterns and sora and king rails. On late afternoons in spring, visit the pools and mudflats to see yellowlegs, sandpipers, killdeer and other shorebirds. Wintering bald eagles feed on fish and injured waterfowl. Watch, too, for white-tailed deer, squirrels, raccoons, muskrat, beaver, mink and coyotes year 'round.

Size: 3,751 acres   **Nearest town:** Elsberry

Location: Travel north of Elsberry on Highway 79 about 7 miles to County Road H. Take County Road 210 east (opposite County Road H) 1.5 miles to the refuge entrance. Refuge roads are muddy at times, so drive cautiously.

Contact: Clarence Cannon National Wildlife Refuge, P.O. Box 88, Annada, MO 63330 (314) 847-2333

Mink travel widely and reside in a series of homes, such as abandoned burrows and hollow trees.

24 Lock and Dam #24

Bald eagles congregate here from mid-November through March to feed on fish and injured waterfowl. Canada geese and several species of ducks stop on their winter migrations, and great blue herons flock to feed along the banks in summer. From the viewing platform you can see wintering eagles and ospreys. Several species of gulls and terns also come in winter to fish and create a ruckus above the open waters at the dam.

Stop by the Clarksville Visitor Center for indoor viewing with spotting scopes and information on current bird sightings. The Missouri Department of Conservation, along with Clarksville and the U.S. Army Corps of Engineers, hosts a bald eagle event each year in late January.

Size: 6 acres   **Nearest town:** Clarksville

Location: In Clarksville, turn east from Highway 79 on Howard Street, then north on Front Street to the lock and dam. The visitor center is located north of Howard Street on Highway 79.

Contact: U.S. Army Corps of Engineers, Riverlands Area Office, P.O. Box 560, Clarksville, MO 63336, (314) 242-3724

25 Lock and Dam #25

View birds that feed and nest along the Mississippi at Lock and Dam # 25, just a short drive from St. Louis. Bald eagles cluster at the river's edge to feed and roost. From a viewing platform, watch for eagles, ducks, geese, terns and gulls feeding along the river in the winter and spring. One overlook gives you a view of the Lock and Dam, while another overlooks the slough and river below the dam.

Sandy Slough, located near the picnic area, is a good viewing spot in spring and summer for killdeer, great blue herons and egrets. Walk up the levee along Sandy Slough to see Canada geese, white-tailed deer, beaver, muskrat and raccoons.

Size: 8 acres   **Nearest town:** Winfield

Location: Travel north on 79 through Winfield to County Road N. Turn east on N, and travel 3 miles. Look for the U.S. Army Corps of Engineers sign at the gravel road entrance on the left.

Contact: U.S. Army Corps of Engineers, Riverlands Area Office, P.O. Box 560, Clarksville, MO 63336, (314) 242-3724

Missouri's most colorful snake, the red milk snake, is secretive and rarely seen in the open. It lives under rocks and logs. Typically, it ranges in length from 21 to 28 inches. At one time, people mistakenly believed this snake had the ability to suck milk from cows – a myth, but the name stuck. Red milk snakes feed on lizards, small snakes and mice.

26 Cuivre River State Park

In the rugged landscape of the Lincoln Hills, Cuivre River State Park has scenic features and wildlife rarely seen in northern Missouri's plains. Ozark species such as ringed salamanders, broadhead skinks and flowering dogwoods are found here. See plants and wildlife in oak woodlands, bottomland forests, prairies, savannas, glades and streams as you hike some of the state park's nine hiking trails winding 24 miles through the park. Watch for songbirds, toads, frogs, salamanders, lizards, turtles, snakes, white-tailed deer and wildflowers while hiking.

Big Sugar Creek is a clear, rocky stream good for viewing minnows and crayfish in spring and fall. Special places in the park include three designated natural areas (pieces of the landscape as it appeared before settlement) and two wild areas. To learn more about Cuivre River, begin with a stop at the visitor center.

Size: 6,350 acres   **Nearest town:** Troy

Location: From Troy, travel east on Highway 47 for 3 miles to Highway 147. Follow 147 north to the visitor center.

Contact: Missouri Department of Natural Resources, Cuivre River State Park, Route 1, Box 25, Troy, MO 63379, (314) 528-7247 or (800) 334-6946

27 Danville and Whetstone Creek Conservation Areas

Danville's rocky meadows or glades come alive with color in spring and fall. Indian paintbrush, pale purple coneflower and prairie grasses grow on the sloping glades. Listen for ruffed grouse drumming early mornings in March or April. Walk the trails, and watch for indigo buntings, blue-winged warblers and other songbirds. You're apt to see lizards and snakes in the rocky forests and glades during the summer.

At Whetstone Creek, the scenic Ozark stream with the same name winds through with long, deep pools broken by riffles and gravel bars. Along the natural area and creek, watch for belted kingfishers and great blue herons. Bluffs above the creek have dogwoods, redbuds and a variety of wildflowers that lend color to spring. In late March and early April, woodcocks perform their evening courtship displays in fields.

Danville Conservation Area

Size: 2,654 acres   **Nearest town:** Kingdom City

Location: From Kingdom City, go east on Interstate 70 for 9 miles to the Danville exit. Turn south on County Road N to the outer road. Turn east on the outer road, and travel 2 miles to County Road RB. Take RB south 2 miles.

Contact: Missouri Department of Conservation, Box 43, Williamsburg, MO 63388, (314) 254-3330

Whetstone Conservation Area

Size: 5,147 acres   **Nearest town:** Kingdom City

Location: From Kingdom City, travel east on Interstate 70 for 13 miles to the Williamsburg exit at County Road D. Turn north on D for 1 mile, then turn north on County Road 1003. Continue north for 1.8 miles to the area headquarters.

Contact: Missouri Department of Conservation, Box 43, Williamsburg, MO 63388, (314) 254-3330

Belted kingfishers often hover over water, dive vertically, and come up with fish or crayfish. They frequently follow a favored route along a lake shore or stream.

Henslow's sparrows rely on running rather than flying to move from place to place. They are secretive, and usually are seen only when they perch and utter their "song"– an insectlike, two-note "tsi-lick."

28 Tucker Prairie

The prairie is a rare piece of the grasslands that once covered northern and western Missouri. Tucker Prairie's hard clay soils grow a variety of striking wildflowers and prairie wildlife. Sedge wrens and Henslow's sparrows are summer songbirds you'll find here. Rough-legged hawks and northern harriers are the most common winter birds of prey. Snoring calls of northern crawfish frogs can be heard on warm spring evenings, especially after a rain.

You'll find more than 250 species of wildflowers and prairie grasses that create spectacular color displays in early spring through fall – from the ragged fringed orchids and blue false indigo to butterfly-weed and blazing star.

The area is managed by the University of Missouri as a research area. Tucker Prairie Nature Trail, marked by posts, is an interpretive trail which highlights the history of the prairie as a research station and explains prairie ecology and management. When you visit, please register at the entrance and take care not to disturb any research markers or equipment.

Size: 146 acres   **Nearest town:** Columbia

Location: From Interstate 70 and U.S. 63 in Columbia, travel east on 70 for 14.8 miles to County Road M (exit 144). Turn south on M, and travel 1.3 miles, then turn east. Travel 1 mile, turn left at Richland Church, and continue 1.3 miles to the entrance.

Contact: University of Missouri, Department of Biological Sciences, 105 Tucker Hall, Columbia, MO 65211, (314) 882-6659

Missouri River Hills

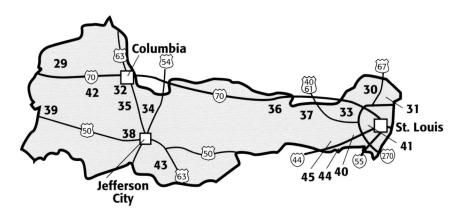

29 Katy Trail State Park
30 Marais Temps Clair
   Conservation Area
31 Riverlands Environmental
   Demonstration Area
32 Rock Bridge Memorial State Park
33 Creve Coeur Park
34 Mark Twain National Forest
   Cedar Creek Trails
35 Three Creeks Conservation Area
36 August A. Busch Memorial
   Conservation Area

37 Dr. Edmund A. Babler
   Memorial State Park
38 Runge Conservation Nature Center
39 Lamine River Conservation Area
40 Queeny Park and Roger Klamberg
   Woods Conservation Area
41 Powder Valley Conservation
   Nature Center
42 Eagle Bluffs Conservation Area
43 Painted Rock Conservation Area
44 Forest 44 Conservation Area
45 West Tyson County Park

Flowing between the Ozark Hills and the Glaciated Plains, waters of the Missouri River carved the countryside. Here, the landscape is cut deeply from sandstone and limestone. Scenic bluffs, pinnacles, caves, springs and sinkholes have been formed by centuries of rolling water.

Forests stretched over the hilltops, along with glades and prairies. The Missouri River once had wide and shallow waters with many channels intertwined – very different from the deep, narrow river of today. Look for swamp white and pin oaks, sugar maples and cottonwoods in the bottomlands. In the uplands, mosses, lichens and ferns grow on the cliffs, while gray fox, southern flying squirrels, eastern chipmunks, pileated woodpeckers and broad-winged hawks live in the dry forests.

Wetlands left behind by the wandering river system are alive in spring and fall with the colors and calls of migrating waterfowl, shorebirds, wading birds and songbirds.

29 Katy Trail State Park

Enjoy the landscape and wildlife along the Missouri River by hiking or biking a trail built on the abandoned MKT railway. The trail is constructed of hard-packed gravel and is wide enough for both hikers and bikers. The river corridor is bounded by crop fields, wetlands, forests, cliffs, springs, caves, prairies and glades. A variety of mammals, songbirds, birds of prey and waterfowl use the habitats along the way.

Watch for herons stalking prey in the backwaters or bald eagles roosting along the bluffs. Along the St. Charles to Marthasville section of the trail, you'll find beautiful bluffs of limestone, dolomite and white sandstone. The Jefferson City to Franklin section also takes you alongside steep bluffs and features Boone Cave, MKT Spring and a roosting site for bald eagles in winter.

Size: Jefferson City to Franklin section – 47 miles; St. Charles to Marthasville section – 35 miles; Boonville to Sedalia section – 33 miles

Nearest towns: St. Charles, Jefferson City and Boonville

Locations: Jefferson City – from the junction of U.S. 54 and U.S. 63 north of Jefferson City, travel southwest on 54/63 for .5 mile to County Road W. Take W northwest .4 mile to Oil Well Road. Travel northeast for .4 mile to Katy Road, then go northeast on Katy Road for .6 mile to the trailhead. St. Charles – take Interstate 70 to 5th Street (exit 229) in St. Charles. Go north on 5th Street for .4 mile, and turn east on Boonslick Road to Riverside Drive. Access to the trailhead and parking is at Frontier Park in St. Charles. Boonville – from Interstate 70 take exit 103, and go north on County Road B for 28 miles to U.S. 40. Take 40 for .3 mile to Spring Street. Turn west on Spring Street, and travel 3.5 blocks to the trail-head south of the street.

Contact:
Missouri Department of Natural Resources, Katy Trail State Park, P.O. Box 176, Jefferson City, MO 65102, (800) 334-6946

Katy Trail State Park — Jefferson City to Franklin Section

Red-tailed hawks soar about 100 feet over open land in search of prey, but also are likely to perch in trees at the edge of a meadow to hunt. They have excellent vision and acuity that allows them to detect the slightest movement great distances away.

30 Marais Temps Clair Conservation Area

As the Missouri River roamed over the years, old channels were abandoned, leaving behind spectacular wetlands such as the oxbow lake at Marais Temps Clair north of St. Louis. To provide habitat for shorebirds and wading birds such as great blue and green herons, snipes and rails, the water levels in the pools are raised at different seasons.

The wetland also attracts migratory waterfowl – thousands of Canada geese and many duck species during spring and fall migration. Watch, too, for two introduced birds, the Eurasian tree sparrow and ring-necked pheasant. Bald eagles congregate around the water in winter, northern harriers migrate through in late summer, and red-tailed hawks and barred owls remain here year 'round. In spring and summer, you'll see turtles, frogs and snakes basking in the sun or feeding near the water's edge. The area is closed to other uses during waterfowl hunting season.

Size: 918 acres   **Nearest town:** St. Charles

Location: From Interstate 70 in St. Charles, take Highway 94 north 8 miles to County Road H. Travel east on H for 1.5 miles to Island Road. Turn north on Island Road 2 miles to the area entrance.

Contact: Missouri Department of Conservation, 2360 Highway D, St. Charles, MO 63304, (314) 441-4554

There are 25 species of gulls in North America and, surprisingly, about 16 of them make an appearance in Missouri at various times of the year. The ring-billed gull is commonly found inland during winter.

31 Riverlands Environmental Demonstration Area

One of the top birding spots in Missouri, Riverlands has four habitats on 1,200 acres of bottomland between the Missouri and Mississippi rivers. In addition to the big rivers, there are small lakes, wet prairies and marshes. Roads through the area follow a long levee dividing 2 miles of riverfront from a wet prairie and a marsh. Area wildlife is accustomed to vehicles on the levee, so your automobile is a good viewing blind.

At the prairie, watch for white-tailed deer, red fox, butterflies and wildflowers. Snipes, yellowlegs and lesser golden plovers can be seen in the marsh, while gulls and waterfowl swim and feed along the river and in Ellis Bay. The gulls include ring-billed, herring, glaucous, Thayer's, Bonaparte's and Franklin's. Thousands of canvasback, redhead, ring-necked and lesser scaup ducks migrate through, along with sea ducks such as buffleheads and common goldeneyes. Watch for northern harriers, short-eared owls and bald eagles. Ellis Bay, Teal Pond and below the dam are good locations to see muskrat, beaver, turtles, fish, frogs and aquatic insects moving and feeding.

Walking the trails and levee roads provides good viewing, but some areas are restricted during various seasons. Watch for special regulations signs.

Size: 1,200 acres   **Nearest town:** St. Louis

Location: From the junction of interstates 70 and 270 in St. Louis, take 270 north 5.3 miles to Highway 67. Follow 67 north 11.3 miles to West Alton. Take the entrance road on the right before crossing the bridge.

Contact: Riverlands Area Office, P.O. Box 337, West Alton, MO 63386, (314) 355-6585

Rock Bridge Memorial State Park

The landscape at Rock Bridge has fascinated visitors for centuries. Caves, sinkholes, natural bridges, underground streams and small springs formed over thousands of years as water dissolved the limestone bedrock. There are five trails at the park, so pick up a map as you enter. Be sure to hike Rock Bridge Trail – a boardwalk that takes you through the woods, to viewing platforms, beneath a large natural bridge and to Devil's Icebox sinkhole cave.

Several species of bats can be seen emerging from the cave entrance at dusk. Little brown, eastern pipistrelle, Indiana and gray bats use the caves. Also watch for marbled and dark-sided salamanders in moist areas along the walkways. To enjoy the scenic features, hike the rugged trails through Gans Creek Wild Area – 750 acres of rugged countryside – and explore the limestone bluffs overlooking Gans Creek.

As you walk the streamside path, watch for belted kingfishers diving for minnows and eastern phoebes chasing insects. White-tailed deer move and feed in the openings at dusk and dawn. In early spring, woodland wildflowers such as bloodroot, trout lily and Dutchman's breeches grow along the wooded trails.

Size: 2,238 acres   **Nearest town:** Columbia

Location: From Columbia at Interstate 70, take Highway 163 (Providence Road) south 7.3 miles to the park entrance.

Contact: Missouri Department of Natural Resources, Rock Bridge Memorial State Park, Columbia, MO 65201, (800) 334-6946

Dog-tooth violets appear from late March to early May. They grow in rich woods, near streams and in lowlands throughout the state.

33 Creve Coeur Park

The Missouri River left behind Creve Coeur Lake when the channel changed hundreds of years ago, closing a bend in the river. At 300 acres, the natural lake attracts migratory waterfowl, wading birds and shorebirds. Winter is the best time to see bald eagles, Canada geese and many species of ducks including mallard, wood, teal, shoveler, bufflehead and merganser.

The west side of the island has a mudflat that attracts shorebirds as well as great blue and green herons and great egrets. Crappie, sunfish, catfish and other river fish are seen in the lake. A few migrating loons stop at the lake each winter. In the woods and throughout the park, watch for bluebirds, warblers, woodpeckers, swallows, belted kingfishers, wild turkeys, American kestrels and red-tailed hawks.

Size: 1,141 acres   **Nearest town:** St. Louis

Location: From the junction of interstates 70 and 270, travel south 3 miles on 270 to Dorsett Road. Travel west on Dorsett for 1 mile to the second park entrance at Marine Avenue on the north side of the road.

Contact: St. Louis County Parks, 41 S. Central Ave., Clayton, MO 63105, (314) 889-2863

Among the puddle ducks or dabblers, the northern shoveler has a most pronounced, specialized bill, which is used for straining plankton and invertebrates from water and mud.

Seeds and buds of poplar and birch trees are the preferred food of ruffed grouse. In spring, the drumming of males can be heard as far as a half-mile away.

34 Mark Twain National Forest
Cedar Creek Trails

Cedar Creek Trails cover 35 miles of grasslands, bluffs, forests and streams. The scenery along Cedar Creek is splendid, especially in spring and fall when the trees lend vibrant colors to the landscape. Prairies and white oak forests border limestone caves and bluffs. Ruffed grouse, white-tailed deer, barred owls and eastern chipmunks are a few of the woodland species you'll find here.

Grasslands and old fields are home to coyotes, bobwhite quail and red-tailed hawks. The trail crosses Cedar Creek – a rocky, winding prairie stream – so watch for Louisiana waterthrushes, belted kingfishers and Acadian flycatchers while you're in the area. Crevices in the bluffs along the stream are nesting spots for rough-winged swallows and eastern phoebes.

Size: 16,000 acres   **Nearest town:** Columbia

Location: From Interstate 70 in Columbia, travel south on U.S. 63 for 12 miles to County Road Y. Travel east on Y for 7 miles to Pine Ridge Campground.

Contact: District Ranger, Mark Twain National Forest, 4965 County Road 304, Fulton, MO 65251, (314) 642-6726

Turkey vultures are experts at "static soaring." By taking advantage of rising warm air and updrafts above hills and bluffs, vultures can stay aloft for hours without a single wing beat.

35 Three Creeks Conservation Area

Situated in scenic river hills, Three Creeks has striking limestone ridges and bluffs carved out of the hillsides. Three creeks – Bass, Bonne Femme and Turkey – wind through the area. From the overlooks, enjoy colorful hardwoods in mid-October, and observe wildlife from the overlooks year 'round. In early March, turkey vultures congregate here as they return from wintering areas, and red-tailed hawks hunt the open areas.

Trails, including the 1.7-mile Turkey Creek Nature Trail (pick up a brochure at the trailhead), take you through forests and grasslands and past streams. Watch for a variety of songbirds year 'round. By hiking in from the south entrance, you can explore Hunter's Cave and see cave wildlife such as little brown and pipistrelle bats, cave salamanders and cave crickets. The cave is closed April 1 through October 31 to protect the wildlife.

Size: 1,277 acres   **Nearest town:** Columbia

Location: From Interstate 70, travel south 7 miles on U.S. 63 to Deer Park, which lies at the junction of Route AB and U.S. 63. Turn west on Deer Park Road, and travel 1.75 miles to the conservation area parking lot.

Contact: Missouri Department of Conservation, 1907 Hillcrest Dr., Columbia, MO 65201, (314) 882-9880

This large wildlife area near St. Louis has a mixture of timber, open fields, streams, springs and lakes. The 8-mile, self-guided auto tour, combined with 5 miles of walking trails, introduce visitors to several habitats and the area's management. There also are 70 miles of open roads on the area.

Watch for white-tailed deer. They're common in the fields and along wooded edges. Wildlife is attracted to the area's 32 lakes and 60 ponds. More than 280 species of birds have been seen on the area, including many species of shorebirds, waterfowl and warblers. Birdwatching is best during spring and fall migrations. Canada geese, mallard ducks and wood ducks nest on the area and can be seen around the Ahden Knight Hampton Refuge.

In spring and summer, watch for turtles basking on logs. East of Lake 33 is a 13-acre shorebird area where spotted sandpipers, plovers, American bitterns and great blue herons wade and feed. To photograph or observe wildlife, there are several upland viewing blinds.

The bridge on Dardenne Creek is a scenic place to see spring and summer wildflowers. The 7,300-acre Weldon Spring Conservation Area is adjacent to the Busch Area. Combined, these areas have more than 20 miles of hiking trails. The Katy Trail (see page 28) also passes through Weldon Spring along the river.

Size: 6,987 acres   **Nearest town:** St. Charles

Location: From the junction of U.S. 40 and Highway 94, turn west on 94, and drive 1 mile to the entrance on the north side of the road. Weldon Spring Conservation Area is located south of the Busch Area on the banks of the Missouri River. Howell Island Conservation Area is a large river island across from Weldon Spring.

Contact: Missouri Department of Conservation, 2360 Highway D, St. Charles, MO 63304, (314) 441-4554

Adult red-eared sliders range in length from five to eight inches. They are found throughout the state except for a few northern border counties.

37 Dr. Edmund A. Babler Memorial State Park

On the rugged hills of Babler Memorial State Park grow lush, old oak and hickory trees. Serviceberry, flowering dogwood, pawpaw and redbud trees scattered through the forest understory provide a vivid spring display. Woodland wildflowers such as white trillium, dog-tooth violet, harbinger of spring and rue anemone also contribute to the spring color. In fall, oaks and maples paint the landscape with fiery fall color.

Watch for hawks, owls, warblers, woodpeckers, wild turkeys and white-tailed deer near the woodlands. Forest mammals, including red fox, gray fox, flying squirrels, eastern chipmunks, raccoons and striped skunks, are seen in the park. Other features are Cochran Hollow Woods and Babler Southwoods Hollow Natural Area – forests with large oak trees that look much like they did before the area was settled. For a better understanding of the forest ecosystems, take time to see the exhibits at the visitor center.

Size: 2,439 acres   **Nearest town:** Chesterfield

Location: From the intersection of U.S. 40/61 and Highway 340 (Clarkson Road), travel south 5 miles to Highway 100 (Manchester Road). Take 100 west 3 miles to Highway 109. Turn north on 109 for 5 miles to the park entrance on the west side of the road.

Contact: Missouri Department of Natural Resources, Babler State Park, 800 Guy Park Dr., Chesterfield, MO 63005, (800) 334-6946

Gray foxes can shift to a meatless diet, eating insects, berries and other plants. They also are able to climb trees, using their claws to climb bear-hug style.

38 Runge Conservation Nature Center

For a quick glimpse of Missouri's wildlife habitats, stop and see the exhibits at Runge Conservation Nature Center. A 3,400-gallon aquarium with fish and turtles awaits you. The nature center features year 'round wildlife viewing, programs and naturalist-led hikes. Seven trails pass through woods and prairie, and near a marsh and ponds. When you visit the small marsh, watch for turtles, frogs and dragonflies. The tallgrass prairie planting is painted pink by blazing stars and pale purple coneflowers in summer, and the native grasses dry golden in fall.

In the woodlands, watch for white-tailed deer or red fox crossing the trail. Bluebirds are active around the nest boxes in summer, and a wildlife feeding station near the building attracts songbirds, eastern chipmunks, fox squirrels and other animals. A landscaped trail in back of the building also shows some methods for attracting wildlife to your backyard.

Size: 97 acres   **Nearest town:** Jefferson City

Location: From the junction of U.S. 63/54 and U.S. 50, travel west 2.8 miles to Highway 179. Turn north on 179, and drive .3 mile to the nature center entrance on the west side of the road.

Contact: Missouri Department of Conservation, Runge Conservation Nature Center, P.O. Box 180, Jefferson City, MO 65102, (314) 526-5544

39 Lamine River Conservation Area

Riverways provide the best wildlife viewing here at the headwaters of the Lamine River, where Richland Creek and Flat Creek meet. The river flows north to the Missouri River and provides a good stretch of water for canoeing and wildlife observation. Pools, riffles and rock bars let you enjoy fish and other water wildlife while you float. River otters and other wetland wildlife are seen in the rivers, ponds and marshes. Watch, too, for songbirds along wooded bluffs, and bobwhite quail, cottontail rabbits, fox squirrels and wild turkeys in the upland areas year 'round. The creeks and rivers also attract bald eagles in winter.

Size: 5,692 acres   **Nearest town:** Sedalia

Location: From the junction of U.S. 50 and U.S. 65 in Sedalia, travel east on 50 for 15.5 miles to the parking area on the north side of the road.

Contact: Missouri Department of Conservation, 1014 Thompson Blvd., Sedalia, MO 65301, (816) 530-5500

Queeny Park and Roger Klamberg Woods Conservation Area

Sweet William grows to about one foot tall April through June, usually in partial or full shade.

For an area with good trails and abundant urban wildlife, visit Queeny Park. Mature forests are mixed with open fields and small ponds. Forested areas are good places to find spring wildflowers, especially along the stream. You can view songbirds such as bluebirds, cardinals and goldfinches most of the year. Many species of warblers stop during spring and fall migrations, and ducks and geese swim on the lakes.

Located in the hills near the Meramec River, Klamberg Woods is home to many songbirds, wildflowers, insects and mammals. Here, a nature trail winds .7 mile through the forest where white oaks tower above, and flowering dogwood, trillium, trout lily and columbine bloom in the spring understory, followed by sweet William, larkspur and mayapple in late spring. Hike the trail at Keifer Creek, watching for salamanders in wet areas, phoebes chasing insects near the water, and crayfish and tadpoles in stream pools as you pass. Viewing platforms on the trail are good spots to stop and look for songbirds and mammals. At both areas, woodpeckers, raccoons, opossums, eastern chipmunks and fox squirrels are active in the woodlands, while white-tailed deer, red fox, wild turkeys, songbirds and butterflies feed in open areas. (Facility symbols apply to Queeny Park..)

Size: Queeny Park, 569 acres; Klamberg Woods, 67 acres

Nearest town: St. Louis

Locations: From the junction of Interstate 270 and Manchester Road, take Manchester west 2.5 miles to Weidman Road. Turn north on Weidman 1 mile to Queeny Park on the east side of the road. Klamberg Woods is 4.6 miles farther west on Manchester Road. Take Highway 340 (Keifer Creek Road) south .7 mile to the Bluebird Park entrance.

Contact for Queeny Park: St. Louis County Parks, 41 S. Central Ave., Clayton, MO 63105, (314) 889-2863

Contact For Klamberg Woods: Ellisville Parks and Recreation, 16 Keifer Creek Rd., Ellisville, MO 63011, (314) 227-7508

41 Powder Valley Conservation Nature Center

At Powder Valley, you'll see many of the natural features once found throughout the St. Louis area. In this remnant of steep, hilly woods, watch for seasonal colors of flowering dogwood, redbud, oak, hickory and maple trees as you walk the trails. More than 2 miles of paved hiking trails take you past woodland wildflowers and rocky shelves on the hillsides.

The nature center features exhibits on plants and wildlife found in urban areas, and a wildlife feeding station where you're sure to see wildlife any time of year. Watch for gray squirrels, cottontail rabbits, raccoons, opossums, eastern chipmunks, wild turkeys, woodpeckers and forest songbirds while visiting the area. You may want to continue your trip by visiting nearby 93-acre Emmenegger Nature Park. From the park trails, you'll also see the Meramec River's forested hills.

Size: 112 acres   **Nearest town:** St. Louis

Location: From Interstate 270, take Interstate 44 east, and exit on Watson Road. Take Watson Road to Geyer Road (first light), then turn left on Geyer, and travel to Cragwold Road (200 yards). Turn left on Cragwold, and follow the road for .5 mile to the entrance road on the right. To reach Emmenegger Nature Park, continue past the nature center entrance.

Contact: Missouri Department of Conservation, Powder Valley Conservation Nature Center, 11715 Cragwold Rd., Kirkwood, MO 63122, (314) 821-8427

An opossum will transport leaves and other nest-building materials in a loop of its tail. If confronted or captured by predators, it will go into a nervous shock and "play dead" until danger passes or it can escape.

42 Eagle Bluffs Conservation Area

Eagle Bluffs is an old river bend with a colorful history and a promising future. Locally known as Plowboy Bend for a steamboat that sank here in the mid-1800s, Eagle Bluffs is now a restored wetland and wastewater treatment wetland.

As the primary wetland in central Missouri, bald eagles and ospreys, shorebirds, waterfowl and herons and egrets all are drawn to the area. On spring mornings, watch for songbirds such as grosbeaks migrating through grasslands and shrubby areas. Bald eagles and ospreys are most abundant in winter along the river shore.

Waterfowl and shorebirds will create the best displays at the pools in spring and fall at dusk and dawn. Herons and egrets are seen in warmer months along the river and in pools. Steep dolomite bluffs rise high above the river bottom for a spectacular view of the muddy Missouri and its wildlife. The Katy Trail (see page 28) also passes through the area. Facilities may vary due to flood reconstruction.

Size: 3,656 acres   **Nearest town:** Columbia

Location: From Interstate 70 in Columbia, travel south on Highway 163 (Providence Road) 5 miles to County Road K. Follow K west 5 miles past McBaine to the area entrance.

Contact: Missouri Department of Conservation, 6700 W. Route K, Columbia, MO 65203, (314) 445-3882

Stilt sandpipers prefer to linger around the edges of ponds and grassy marshes. They often are seen with yellowlegs and dowitchers.

Scientists recognize 3,307 species of lizards in the world. Missouri's 10 species of lizards, including the northern fence lizard, are nonvenomous and beneficial because they eat a variety of insects.

43 Painted Rock Conservation Area

On the wooded bluffs above the Osage River, Painted Rock offers beautiful river scenery and excellent wildlife viewing. Trails in the area wind up and down the forested river hills, offering spectacular views of fall color during mid-October. Osage Bluff Scenic Trail is 1.6 miles along high river bluffs and through an oak-hickory-sugar maple forest. Observation decks on the bluffs give you a scenic view of the Osage River.

While you're enjoying the landscape, watch for turkey vultures in spring and summer, and bald eagles in winter. Where the trail drops down to the river bottom, watch for woodland songbirds and enjoy trillium, bloodroot and other wildflowers in spring. As the trail skirts the river bluff and crosses an open, glade-like forest, watch for white-tailed deer, wild turkeys, fence lizards and fox squirrels moving across the forest floor in spring and summer. Hike other trails on the area to see more of the bluffs and river.

Size: 1,480 acres   **Nearest town:** Jefferson City

Location: From Jefferson City, travel east on U.S. 50 for 7 miles to U.S. 63 south. Follow 63 south 3 miles to Highway 133. Take 133 south 6.5 miles to the first entrance on the right.

Contact: Missouri Department of Conservation, P.O. Box 1128 (12655 State Route Y), Rolla, MO 65401, (314) 368-2225

44 Forest 44 Conservation Area

Close to urban St. Louis, Forest 44 is a welcome outdoor retreat. In spring, the area blooms with flowering dogwood and redbud, while fall brings spectacular color to the rugged landscape. Hiking and equestrian trails cover much of the area. From trails and viewing platforms, watch for songbirds such as bluebirds and goldfinches and large numbers of migrating hawks flying over in spring and fall.

Salamanders, including tiger, marbled and spotted, are found in moist woodlands and around ponds. From a boardwalk and deck on one of the area's 12 ponds, listen for the calls of toads and frogs in spring. Barred owls call in the forests at sunrise and sunset from late winter through spring. You also can see red-tailed hawks and white-tailed deer throughout the area.

Size: 958 acres   **Nearest town:** St. Louis

Location: From the junction of interstates 270 and 44, travel west on 44 for 3.5 miles to Highway 141. Travel south on 141 to Meramec Station Road (first stoplight) and turn right. Follow Meramec Station Road west .9 mile to Hillsboro Road. Turn left on Hillsboro for .4 mile to the parking area on the right.

Contact: Missouri Department of Conservation, 2751 Glencoe Rd., Glencoe, MO 63038, (314) 458-2236

45 West Tyson County Park

Located in the wooded hills above the Meramec River, West Tyson County Park is one of the largest St. Louis County parks. Rugged hills and valleys host rich hardwood forests and an abundance of wildlife. You can see wild turkeys, fox and gray squirrels and red fox in wooded areas. Bluebirds and coyotes live in the grasslands, and herons, beaver and muskrat are found along the river.

Chubb Trail is a 7-mile hiking trail that links West Tyson Park with Castlewood State Park and Lone Elk County Park to the east. The hiking and equestrian trail is a very rough, yet scenic path through the hills and river valley. You also can enjoy river wildlife by canoeing this stretch of the Meramec River.

Size: 668 acres   **Nearest town:** St. Louis

Location: From the intersection of interstates 270 and 44, take 44 west 10 miles to North Outer Road (exit 265). Continue west on North Outer Road .1 mile.

Contact: St. Louis County Parks, 41 S. Central Ave., Clayton, MO 63105, (314) 889-2863

Osage Plains

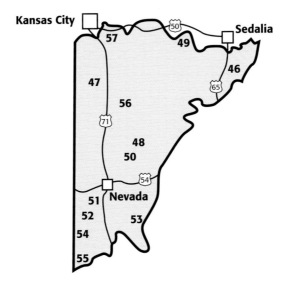

46 Paint Brush Prairie, Friendly Prairie and Grandfather Prairie Conservation Areas

47 Bittern Bottoms and Dorsett Hill Prairie Conservation Areas

48 Taberville Prairie Conservation Area

49 Knob Noster State Park

50 Schell-Osage and Four Rivers Conservation Areas

51 Osage Prairie and Little Osage Prairie Conservation Areas

52 Bushwhacker Lake Conservation Area

53 Stony Point Prairie and Niawathe Prairie Conservation Areas

54 Prairie State Park

55 Wah-Sha-She Prairie Conservation Area

56 Settle's Ford Conservation Area

57 James A. Reed Memorial Wildlife Area

Great herds of bison and elk once grazed the gently rolling Osage Plains. The tallgrass prairie, mixed with savanna and forest, is no longer home to bison and wolves, but you'll enjoy the color and splendor of the grassland fragments that remain.

The prairies are rich with grasses and wildflowers. Tickseed coreopsis, downy sunflower, Indian paintbrush, lousewort, shooting star, coneflower, wild indigo and goldenrod give color to little and big bluestem and Indian grass.

Many animals of the area have adapted well to life in the sea of grass. Badger, gopher, ground squirrel and several kinds of mice make burrows in the ground. Northern harrier, prairie chicken, upland sandpiper, short-eared owl, dickcissel and scissor-tailed flycatcher fly and feed across the prairie.

Before European settlement, more than two-thirds of the prairie was mixed with savanna and forest, while the stream valleys were broad and shallow with many spectacular wetlands.

Naturalist Aldo Leopold said in 1938, "Until a majority of our farmers are as proud of having a flock of prairie chickens as of owning a new car, we shall not have the chickens." Once plentiful, the birds declined over the years as prairies were converted for agriculture and other uses. There are fewer than 3,000 prairie chickens remaining in Missouri.

Paint Brush Prairie, Friendly Prairie and Grandfather Prairie Conservation Areas

To see grasslands as they appeared centuries ago, visit one of these tallgrass prairies. If you visit in the spring, don't be surprised to see parts of the prairie blackened by fire. Controlled burning is used to help maintain the natural character of the prairies. You won't find developed trails on these areas, so hike cross-country and experience the prairie as Native Americans and European settlers once did.

Greater prairie chicken, wild turkey and bobwhite quail feed and nest in the grasses, while upland sandpiper and woodcock call and perform their courtship flights on spring evenings. An unusual animal – the prairie mole cricket – also can be heard in late April. Listen for its droning at Paint Brush after sundown.

The most spectacular display on the prairies is the wildflowers during spring and summer. Pale purple coneflower, coreopsis, blazing star, Indian paintbrush and many other blooms blanket the ridge tops in red, yellow, pink and white. Watch for skipper, regal fritillary and other butterflies gathering nectar in spring and fall. While you walk the

Indian paintbrush found in Missouri is mostly red and occasionally yellow. Plants grow eight to 15 inches tall.

ridges, you may discover coyotes and other mammals, winter raptors such as northern harriers, and songbirds such as scissor-tailed flycatchers, dickcissels and Henslow's sparrows. Watch, too, for reptiles such as box turtles, glass lizards and bullsnakes. Part of Paint Brush Prairie is a Designated Natural Area.

Size: Paint Brush Prairie, 314 acres; Friendly Prairie, 40 acres; Grandfather Prairie, 78 acres

Nearest town: Sedalia

Locations: From the junction of U.S. 50 and U.S. 65 in Sedalia, travel south on 65 for 11 miles. Turn east on a gravel road approximately .1 mile to Paint Brush Prairie's parking lot on the north side of the road. Friendly Prairie is located on the same gravel road west of U.S. 65. Travel 1.4 miles to the parking lot on the north side of the road. Friendly Prairie is owned by the Missouri Prairie Foundation and managed by the Missouri Department of Conservation. Grandfather Prairie is 9.9 miles south of Sedalia on U.S. 65. At the gravel road, travel 1.7 miles west to the parking lot.

Contact: Missouri Department of Conservation, 1014 Thompson Blvd., Sedalia, MO 65301, (816) 530-5500

A member of the heron family, least bitterns are small, elusive and secretive. They run and climb quickly through cattails and reeds and have vertical color patterns to help keep them hidden.

47 Bittern Bottoms and Dorsett Hill Prairie Conservation Areas

A variety of shorebirds and waterfowl stop here during migration, making this small marsh a favorite among Missouri birdwatchers. Bittern Bottoms, located in the bottomland of the South Grand River, is named for the least bittern that often nests in the marsh. For the best viewing, hike from the road to the circular levee. You may see wood ducks, blue-winged teal and mallards in the open water.

American and least bitterns, prothonotary warblers and tree swallows all nest in the marsh and feed in the sedge meadow along the west edge of the area. Watch, too, for wading birds and marsh songbirds. A few miles south of Bittern Bottoms, you'll find Dorsett Hill Prairie Conservation Area – a prairie knoll where prairie birds feed, including long-eared owls, in late winter.

Size: Bittern Bottoms, 67 acres; Dorsett Hill, 79 acres

Nearest town: Harrisonville

Locations: From the junction of Highway 2 and U.S. 71 in Harrisonville, travel west on 2 for 2.3 miles to County Road DD. Turn south and drive 6.4 miles on DD to its intersection with 307 Street. Travel east on 307 Street, and continue .5 mile to the parking lot located on the north side of the road. Dorsett Hill Prairie Conservation Area is south of Bittern Bottoms. From Harrisonville, travel south on U.S. 71 for 11 miles. At Archie, turn west on County Road A for 4.5 miles, and turn north on County Road W for 1 mile. Where the highway turns west, continue north on Dorsett Hill Road for .8 mile, and turn east on 333 Street for .5 mile to the prairie on the east side of the road.

Contact: Missouri Department of Conservation, 722 E. Highway 54, Box 106, El Dorado Springs, MO 64744, (417) 876-5226

48 Taberville Prairie Conservation Area

At Taberville Prairie, you'll find grassland songbirds along the scenic prairie ridges, sandstone outcrops, prairie mounds and prairie stream. One of Missouri's largest prairie chicken populations lives here. Watch, too, for hawks, owls, upland sandpipers and other birds. Prairie wildflowers and native grasses create a lush and colorful landscape. During your visit, be sure to walk along the small prairie stream and look in the pools for frogs, fish, crayfish and insects. Part of Taberville Prairie is a Designated Natural Area.

Size: 1,680 acres   **Nearest town:** El Dorado Springs

Location: From El Dorado Springs, travel north on Highway 82 for 2 miles north to County Road H. Take H north for 11 miles through Taberville to the parking area to the east.

Contact: Missouri Department of Conservation, 722 E. Highway 54, Box 106, El Dorado Springs, MO 64744, (417) 876-5226

49 Knob Noster State Park

The grassland and savanna landscape is returning to Knob Noster State Park. Clearfork Creek winds through the center of the park, with a wide band of trees on the banks. Where the forest meets prairie, there lies a savanna or grassland with scattered trees. Seven trails loop through the area. Along the trails, watch for great blue herons near the creek, pileated woodpeckers and barred owls in the forests, and white-tailed deer, red fox, raccoons and wild turkeys along the forest edges and savannas.

The 2-mile North Loop Trail circles a stand of tallgrass prairie where sensitive brier, black-eyed Susan and blazing star bloom. Pin Oak Slough Natural Area is an old creek bed of Clearfork Creek. Here, the oxbow has grown up with maples and oaks – a good spot for watching songbirds. Clearfork savanna is a scenic grassland dotted with oaks, an example of the area's natural character before settlement. The park visitor center focuses on the natural features of the area.

Size: 3,600 acres   **Nearest town:** Knob Noster

Location: From U.S. 50 in Knob Noster, travel west to Highway 132. Travel south on 132 for 1 mile to the park entrance.

Contact: Missouri Department of Natural Resources, Knob Noster State Park, Knob Noster, MO 65336, (800) 334-6946

50 Schell-Osage and Four Rivers Conservation Areas

At Schell-Osage, you'll find a large waterfowl area with rich bottomlands of oak, hickory and pecan trees and natural oxbow sloughs along the Osage River. In spring and fall, white pelicans, waterfowl and shorebirds are spectacular as they fly in to rest and feed during migration. Bald eagles arrive in late December and stay until February, feeding on fish and injured waterfowl. The goose population swells to several thousand in fall when migrating snow and Canada geese arrive.

Watch for family groups of otters on the wetland's frozen ponds and lakes in winter. Peregrine falcons appear annually following the duck migration. Among the wading birds, you'll see great blue herons fishing along the water's edge in summer. Prairie remnants within Schell-Osage have been designated a natural area.

Four Rivers is located in the bottomlands along the Marmaton, Little Osage, Osage and Marais des Cygnes rivers. The four tracts of land have wet prairies, savannas, forests and wetlands. In the woodlands, you'll find white-tailed deer, coyotes, fox and songbirds, as well as many small mammals. Watch for signs of bobcats, too, while walking through woods. Frogs, turtles, snakes, fish, insects, wading birds and aquatic mammals commonly are seen along the rivers.

Schell-Osage Conservation Area

Size: 8,633   **Nearest town:** Nevada

Location: Travel east on U.S. 54 from the junction of U.S. 71 and 54 in Nevada. Take 54 east 14.4 miles to County Road AA. Turn north on AA, and drive 11 miles to County Road RA. Travel east on RA, and continue 1.5 miles to the area headquarters.

Contact: Missouri Department of Conservation, 722 E. Highway 54, Box 106, El Dorado Springs, MO 64744, (417) 876-5226

Four Rivers Conservation Area

Size: 6,696 acres   **Nearest town:** Nevada

Location: Take Highway 71 north from Nevada 16 miles to County Road TT. Turn east on TT, and travel 1.2 miles to the second gravel road on the south. Take the gravel road south for 1.9 miles to the area headquarters.

Contact: Missouri Department of Conservation, 722 E. Highway 54, Box 106, El Dorado Springs, MO 64744, (417) 876-5226

51 Osage Prairie and Little Osage Prairie Conservation Areas

To see one of the largest prairies in Missouri, along with wildlife and elegant grasses and wildflowers of the plains, visit Osage Prairie and Little Osage Prairie conservation areas. The prairie is a mix of grasses, wildflowers and shrubs that provides habitat for prairie chicken, Henslow's sparrow, upland sandpiper and many other grassland songbirds. In March and April, listen for the booming call of male prairie chickens as they compete for a mate.

Watch for songbirds, northern harrier and scissor-tailed flycatcher in the spring while you hike across the prairie. You may see a coyote, red fox or badger crossing in the distance. Short-eared owls migrate south and hunt on the prairie in winter.

When the pale purple coneflower and butterfly weed bloom in June and July, thousands of regal fritillary butterflies dot the prairie. Come fall, you'll enjoy the golden display of big and little bluestem grasses, Indian grass, switch grass, prairie dropseed and wild rye. All of Little Osage Prairie and part of Osage Prairie are designated natural areas.

Size: Osage Prairie, 1,546 acres; Little Osage Prairie, 80 acres

Nearest town: Nevada

Locations: From Nevada, travel south 6 miles on U.S. 71 to the gravel road west of the junction of County Road E. Turn west on the gravel road, and travel 1.7 miles to the second gravel road on the south. Turn south and drive .6 mile to the Osage Prairie parking area on the east side of the road. Little Osage Prairie is 1.5 miles west on the gravel road that lies west of the junction of County Road E. Turn north on the second gravel road to the parking lot on the west side of the road. Little Osage Prairie is owned by The Nature Conservancy and managed by the Missouri Department of Conservation.

Contact: Missouri Department of Conservation, 722 E. Highway 54, Box 106, El Dorado Springs, MO 64744, (417) 876-5226

Orange spots and shimmering blue-green colors of the blue swallowtail butterfly are a warning to would-be predators that this species contains acrid body juices.

52 Bushwhacker Lake Conservation Area

Bushwhacker was once tallgrass prairie, with timbered draws and streams, and today, you can still enjoy the prairies and meadows of blooming wildflowers from early spring until the first frost. Lakes and ponds on the area, including 157-acre Bushwhacker Lake, attract hundreds of waterfowl in spring and fall, as well as white-tailed deer, raccoons and wild turkeys year 'round.

Prairie wildlife inhabit the area. Watch for signs of prairie chickens, badgers, bobcats and coyotes. A flock of about 75 greater prairie chickens lives in the western part of Bushwhacker. Northern harriers are seen year 'round and in early December, Cooper's, sharp-shinned and other migrating hawks soar above the area.

Size: 4,217 acres **Nearest town:** Nevada

Location: Travel west from Nevada 3.2 miles on U.S. 54 to Highway 43. Turn south on 43, and drive 13.4 miles to the directional sign at a gravel road that forms the Vernon and Barton county line. Turn east on the gravel road, and drive 1.8 miles to the second parking area on the north side of the road.

Contact: Missouri Department of Conservation, 2630 N. Mayfair, Springfield, MO 65803, (417) 895-6880

Coyotes are efficient scavengers as well as hunters. In addition to capturing rodents and rabbits, they will eat berries, nuts, fruits, insects, frogs and turtles.

When an upland sandpiper alights, it holds its wings over its back before folding them down in a resting position. Listen for its whistling trills and wind-like sounds. Also known as grass plovers, upland sandpipers once were hunted for food and sport until they became scarce. Today they are protected.

53 Stony Point Prairie and Niawathe Prairie Conservation Areas

Sandstone ledges jut out of the prairie ridges at Stony Point. Both Stony Point and Niawathe, which is a Designated Natural Area, have spectacular blooms of prairie wildflowers in spring and early summer. Expect to see the area vibrantly colored with Indian paintbrush, lousewort, coreopsis, shooting star, wild hyacinth, bird's-foot violet, toadflax, hoary puccoon, false indigo and many other showy wildflowers.

In March and April, listen for greater prairie chickens calling in early morning and evening. Upland sandpipers, northern harriers and Henslow's sparrows feed and call on the prairies too. To enjoy the prairie landscape, wildflowers and wildlife, try cross-country hiking at either of these prairies.

Size: Stony Point Prairie, 640 acres; Niawathe Prairie, 320 acres

Nearest town: Lamar

Locations: Stony Point – travel east from Lamar on U.S. 160 for 9 miles to County Road E. Take E for 4 miles to County Road D. Turn north on D, and go 3 miles to the parking lot on the left. Niawathe Prairie – located off County Road E, 3 miles east of the junction of county roads D and E. On the third gravel road, turn north .5 mile.

Contact: Missouri Department of Conservation, 2360 N. Mayfair, Springfield, MO 65803, (417) 895-6880

54 Prairie State Park

Bison and elk once again graze the tall grasses at Prairie State Park. Use caution when viewing bison, and watch them from your vehicle only. For the location of the bison and to learn of other recent natural events, stop by the visitor center. The facility showcases the history and ecology of Missouri tallgrass prairie.

In early April, greater prairie chickens strut and call to attract a mate. There are several leks, or booming grounds, in the park where you can watch males sparring and defending their territories. Henslow's sparrow, scissor-tailed fly-catcher, dickcissel, kingbird, northern harrier and upland sandpiper are common summer birds of the park. Watch, too, for box turtles, glass lizards, bull-snakes and other prairie reptiles in summer.

More than 10 miles of trails take you past prairie streams with clear waters, scenic sandstone outcrops and many aquatic animals. Be sure you take time to enjoy the prairie streams – East Drywood Creek is especially rich in prairie fish. More than 300 species of wildflowers color the prairie from early spring through late fall. In early summer, monarch, regal fritillary, skipper and many other butterflies fly over the prairie, stopping among the coneflower and blazing star.

Keep an eye out for white-tailed deer and coyote. Burrows or holes in the ground may belong to a badger, prairie crayfish, prairie vole or one of many other prairie animals that make a home underground. Prairie State Park has designated natural areas: Tzi-Sho and Hunkah prairies and East Drywood Creek.

Size: 3,302 acres   **Nearest town:** Lamar

Location: From Lamar, travel west on U.S. 160 for 10 miles to Highway 43. Turn north on 43 for 5 miles to County Road K. Follow K west 4 miles to the intersection of County Road P. Turn west on P for 2 miles to a gravel road to the south (NW 150th Lane). Drive south 1.5 miles to the visitor center.

Contact: Missouri Department of Natural Resources, Prairie State Park, Liberal, MO 64762, (800) 334-6946

Badgers use powerful front claws and feet to dig ground squirrels out of their underground homes and to capture rabbits and other rodents for food.

Sedge wrens, formerly called short-billed marsh wrens, are probably the hardest wrens to spot. They are shy and secretive. A male builds several nests in its territory, only one of which will be chosen by a female for nesting. This contributes to the difficulty in locating and accurately counting their populations.

55 Wah-Sha-She Prairie Conservation Area

A marsh at Wah-Sha-She adds wetland plants and wildlife to the wealth of the prairie. At the 10-acre marsh and pond complex, you'll see reptiles and amphibians native to prairie marshes, plus shorebirds, ducks and wading birds. You'll hear the booming call of prairie chickens in April, and watch for lesser golden plovers, upland sandpipers, American pipits and Henslow's sparrows spring to summer.

Shooting star, Indian paintbrush, cream wild indigo and other spring wildflowers paint the landscape in April and May, giving way to coreopsis, pale purple coneflower and blazing star in June and July. If you visit Wah-Sha-She in the fall, watch for terns, pelicans, cormorants, ducks, and snow, Canada and white-fronted geese. In fall and winter, look for birds of prey soaring above the prairie. Wah-Sha-She Prairie is a Designated Natural Area.

Size: 160 acres   **Nearest town:** Joplin

Location: From the junction of highways 43 and 171 in Joplin, travel on 171 northwest for 10.8 miles to County Road M. Turn east on M, and drive 1 mile to the first gravel road to the north. Turn north on the gravel road, and drive .2 mile to the parking lot on the west side of the road. Wah-Sha-She Prairie is owned by The Nature Conservancy and managed by the Missouri Department of Conservation.

Contact: Missouri Department of Conservation, 2630 N. Mayfair, Springfield, MO 65803, (417) 895-6880

56 Settle's Ford Conservation Area

To view river wildlife and migratory birds, visit Settle's Ford and hike the levees. The South Grand River flows through the center of Settle's Ford, so you can walk along the river levees to see beaver, mink, herons, belted kingfishers, red-eared slider and map turtles, frogs and aquatic insects. From November to March, watch for waterfowl in the bottomlands and shallow water as you travel the roadways. Bald eagles feed along the river from early December to the end of January.

Size: 6,578 acres   **Nearest town:** Harrisonville

Location: From the junction of U.S. 71 and Highway 7 south of Harrisonville, take 7 east 10 miles to Garden City. Turn south on County Road F for 6 miles to County Road B. Go east on B to the area entrance at Index Road. Follow Index Road south to the first parking area on the left.

Contact: Missouri Department of Conservation, 722 E. Highway 54, Box 106, El Dorado Springs, MO 64744, (417) 876-5226

57 James A. Reed Memorial Wildlife Area

Waterfowl, shorebirds and wading birds come to this area's many lakes. A marsh and 12 lakes cover more than 250 acres. Watch for Canada and snow geese and mallard, goldeneye and canvasback ducks during winter. Waterfowl usually gather on the lakes and are viewed easily from the roadways. In spring and fall, shorebirds feed in the shallow waters, and summer brings herons to wade and feed in the marsh and along the shorelines.

The area is at the north edge of the Osage Plains, so you can hike trails through prairies, forests and an array of habitats. Shawnee Trace Nature Trails, located south of Bodarc Lake, are 2.75 miles of trails along Big Creek, forests, cliffs, a limestone glade and rocky slope. Near the creek, watch for white-tailed deer, and stop to enjoy the ancient black walnut and chinquapin oak trees.

Size: 2,456 acres   **Nearest town:** Kansas City

Location: From the junction of Interstate 435 and U.S. 71 in Kansas City, travel east on Interstate 470/U.S. 50 for 7 miles to the U.S. 50 exit. Take U.S. 50 east 5 miles to County Road RA (Ranson Road). Turn south on RA 1.5 miles to the area entrance.

Contact: Missouri Department of Conservation, 13101 Ranson Rd., Lee's Summit, MO 64082, (816) 524-1656

Mississippi River Hills

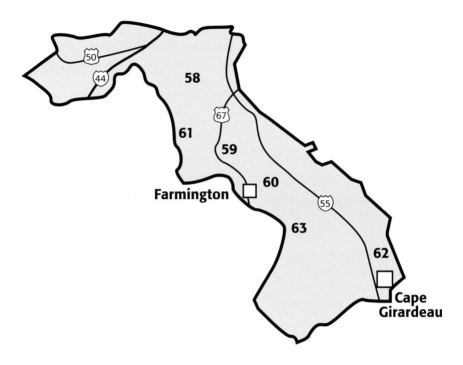

58 Valley View Glades Natural Area
59 St. Francois State Park
60 Pickle Springs Natural Area
 and Hawn State Park

61 Washington State Park
62 Trail of Tears State Park
63 Amidon Memorial
 Conservation Area

The Mississippi River, as it flows south of the Missouri River, is bounded by hills and plains. The Mississippi, too, once had wide waters with many twisting channels much like the Missouri River, except the Mississippi was deeper and broader. Today, the river is deep and narrow, its waters calmed by dams and pools. The Great Flood of `93 gave us a new appreciation for the troubles of this mighty river and a chance to improve the resource.

Rising above the Mississippi are deeply cut hills covered with forests. Rock formations, such as bluffs, pinnacles, caves, sinkholes, glades and canyons, have been created by water and weather erosion. While visiting the region, you'll find rich woodlands with lush ferns and many species of songbirds. Prairie grasses and wildflowers grow on the rocky glades, providing habitat for fence and collared lizards and many kinds of butterflies.

58 Valley View Glades Natural Area

A landscape of glades – dry areas with exposed rocks and thin soils – gives Valley View Glades an unusual array of plants and animals. The exposed rock is dolomite, a dark limestone containing magnesium. A rough trail leads to open rocky slopes of prairie grasses. Stands of post oak, eastern red cedar, flowering dogwood and sumac trees grow in the ravines. Watch for six-lined racerunner, fence and eastern collared lizards sunning on rocks.

Butterfly weed, Missouri evening primrose and black-eyed Susan bloom in early summer, attracting glade grasshoppers and many species of butterflies. You'll see grassland songbirds such as prairie warblers, field sparrows and red-eyed vireos. Near ravines and along the forest edge, watch for white-tailed deer. After a spring rain, the small streams become cascading waterfalls, spilling over ledges and rocks, creating small pools.

Size: 227 acres   **Nearest town:** Hillsboro

Location: From the intersection of Highway 21 and County Road B in Hillsboro, turn west on B, and drive 4.5 miles to the entrance on the north side of the road.

Contact: Missouri Department of Conservation, 2751 Glencoe Rd., Glencoe, MO 63038, (314) 458-2236

Six-lined racerunners are slender, fast-moving lizards which live in open areas. They range in length from six to nine and a half inches and are active on sunny, warm days between 8 a.m. and 3 p.m. Racerunners sometimes are called "fieldstreaks" or "sandlappers."

Be sure to check the back of this book for suggested titles of field guides. Taking a guide book along on your trip will help you identify unfamiliar animals, butterflies or plants, such as grass pink (left) or queen-of-the-prairie (below).

59 St. Francois State Park

At the fens, clear-running streams, glades and forests of St. Francois State Park, you'll experience rare habitats and wildlife. Scenic trails and unusual natural communities include Mooner's Hollow Trail, a 3-mile loop through Coonville Creek Natural Area. While traveling along Coonville Creek, stop at a clear pool to see colorful fish, such as southern redbelly dace, orangethroat darter and slender madtom. Watch for warblers along the trail on spring mornings.

A fen – or wet meadow – is a delicate and rare Ozark habitat found in the Wild Area and the natural area. Here, queen-of-the-prairie, bog coneflower and mountain mint bloom in summer. Spotted salamander, central newt and other amphibians live in the fens and spring branches. In the low woods, celandine poppies flower bright yellow, and bluebells bloom nearby. Swimming Deer Trail loops 2.7 miles through forested hillsides, offering scenic views from the bluffs of Big River.

Size: 2,734 acres

Nearest town: Bonne Terre

Location: Travel north from Bonne Terre 5 miles on U.S. 67 to the park entrance on the east side of the road.

Contact: Missouri Department of Natural Resources, St. Francois State Park, Bonne Terre, MO 63628, (800) 334-6946

Maidenhair ferns grow in moist, shaded ravines and on wooded slopes. They can be found throughout the state, except for the Bootheel.

60 Pickle Springs Natural Area and Hawn State Park

The waters of Pickle Springs flow through enchanting natural areas and a state park, dense with rare plants, animals and geologic features. Hike the Trail Through Time at Pickle Springs Natural Area for a 2-mile journey past waterfalls, rock shelters, a double arch, towering bluffs, canyons and amazing rock outcrops. Spring is the best time to see waterfalls and wild azaleas, which bloom at both areas. During the summer, rattlesnake plantain and six other orchids, partridge berry, farkleberry and lowbush blueberry bloom and display their fruit.

During your visit, notice the shortleaf pine, Missouri's only native pine tree. Moist soils along Pickle and Bone creeks and River aux Vases grow many ferns and rare plants, including cinnamon fern, maidenhair fern, hay-scented fern and club moss. Woodland songbirds move about in the trees and shrubs along the trail. Watch for fence lizards, five-lined skinks, box turtles and leopard frogs among the rocks in summer. From the scenic hiking trails, you can enjoy the splendor of the plants and animals without harming the delicate landscape.

At Hawn State Park, hike the trail to see an area that follows the creek valley past rough, broken hillsides with crystalline rocks exposed by years of fast running waters. Pickle Creek is a clear stream with many fish, such as rainbow darters and striped shiners.

Whispering Pine Trail meanders 10 miles through a 2,080-acre forested wild area. The predominantly pine-oak forest also contains flowering dogwood, sweet gum and sassafras trees. While on the trail, watch for many species of songbirds, especially tanagers and warblers. Wild turkeys, white-tailed deer, raccoons, gray squirrels and owls also are seen along the trails.

Pickle Springs Natural Area

Size: 262 acres   **Nearest town:** Farmington

Location: From the junction of Highway 32 and County Road W in Farmington, travel east on 32 for 5 miles to County Road AA. Turn east on AA for 1.7 miles to Dorlac Road. Turn north on Dorlac Road, and travel .4 mile to the area entrance.

Contact: Missouri Department of Conservation, 2206 W. St. Joseph St., Perryville, MO 63775, (314) 547-4537

Hawn State Park

Size: 4,642 acres   **Nearest town:** Farmington

Location: From the junction of Highway 32 and County Road W in Farmington, travel east on 32 for 10 miles to Highway 144. Take 144 south 4 miles to the park entrance.

Contact: Missouri Department of Natural Resources, Hawn State Park, Ste. Genevieve, MO 63670, (800) 334-6946

Benjamin Franklin proposed that the wild turkey be named our national bird, rather than the bald eagle. In the 1950s, there was a population of only about 2,500 turkeys in Missouri. Thanks to conservation efforts and research, the spring breeding population now is estimated at 380,000.

61 Washington State Park

Washington State Park lies in a region of wooded hills, open glades and clear Ozark streams. You'll enjoy the park's natural communities, cultural features, recreation areas and hiking trails. Stones make the 1,000 Step Trail, which meanders 1.5 miles through Washington Upland Hardwoods Natural Area and along a rocky, forested hillside of towering trees overlooking Big River.

Dutchman's breeches, bloodroot and spring beauty bloom in early spring and color the forest floor. Later in the season, ferns, purple trillium and celandine poppy make up the forest carpet. There are dry, rocky glades on slopes throughout the park. Rockywood Trail is a 10-mile clamber over glades, along high ridges and through wooded hollows. Glade species to see along the way include eastern collared and fence lizards, coachwhip snakes and prairie grasses and wildflowers.

Size: 1,415 acres   **Nearest town:** De Soto

Location: From De Soto, travel south on Highway 21 for 9 miles to Highway 104. Turn north on 104 to the park entrance.

Contact: Missouri Department of Natural Resources, Washington State Park, De Soto, MO 63020, (800) 334-6946

Dutchman's breeches need humus-rich soil and excellent drainage. Look for them along streams, in rich woodlands and below bluffs.

Raccoons hunt cray-fish, frogs and fish in water. On land, they search for worms, snails, grasses, fruit and nuts – especially corn. They also raid strawberry patches. Raccoons have sensitive, hand-like front feet and often put their food in water before eating it.

62 Trail of Tears State Park

The sharp, steep hills along the Mississippi River here look much the same as when the Cherokees passed in 1838 on the "Trail of Tears." Towering river bluffs, deep ravines and densely timbered bottomland border the Mississippi River. The forests are made up of beech and tulip poplar trees – a rare forest in Missouri and more common to the Appalachian Mountains.

Vancill Hollow Natural Area contains a beautiful forest of American beech, tulip poplar and cucumber magnolia trees with wildflowers and ferns on the forest floor. Overlooks and parking areas along the park roads offer scenic bluff-top views of the Mississippi River. Trees on the river bluffs are roosts for wintering bald eagles, and Mississippi kites nest in the tops of cottonwood and sycamore trees in summer. Watch, too, for gulls along the river in winter.

The fall color display in the park is striking. Hike Peewah Trail and enjoy the 10-mile path through Indian Creek Wild Area along wooded ravines and narrow ridges. While hiking, watch for wild turkey, woodland songbirds, white-tailed deer, raccoon, opossum and for signs of bobcat.

Size: 3,306 acres　　　　　**Nearest town:** Cape Girardeau

Location: From Cape Girardeau, take Highway 177 north 12 miles to the park entrance. Turn east on the entrance road, and find the visitor's center on the north side of the road.

Contact: Missouri Department of Natural Resources, Trail of Tears State Park, Jackson, MO 63755, (800) 334-6946

The Castor River has taken hundreds of thousands of years to carve a path through ancient volcanic rock.

63 Amidon Memorial Conservation Area

Missouri's landscape rarely lacks drama, especially at the pink granite shut-ins on the Castor River. The 1-mile Cedar Glade Trail will take you to the shut-ins – a term for igneous rock carved by river waters, creating swift eddies and confusing currents. Near the river, look for mink, raccoon, little blue heron and belted kingfisher, along with buttonbush, pawpaw and witch hazel, which grows along the water and blooms in January and February.

The trail then goes to glades where prairie grasses and wildflowers grow on the granite landscape. Here, watch for reptiles such as eastern collared and fence lizards, as well as songbirds, wild turkey, coyote and white-tailed deer.

Castor River Shut-ins Natural Area is 209 acres in the north half of the conservation area. If you hike to the natural area, you'll find forests of oak and natural pine stands. Forest wildlife includes bobcat, fox and gray squirrels and pileated woodpecker. Glades are scattered on the area and provide good openings for viewing wildlife.

Size: 1,630 acres   **Nearest town:** Fredericktown

Location: Travel east of Fredericktown on Highway 72, and go 2 miles to Highway J. Travel east on J for 4 miles to the junction of Highway W. Turn south on W for 1.3 miles until the pavement ends at County Road 208. Turn left on 208 for 1.1 miles to County Road 253, then turn north .9 mile to the parking area and trailhead on the right.

Contact: Missouri Department of Conservation, 2206 W. St. Joseph, Perryville, MO 63775, (314) 547-4537

Springfield Plateau

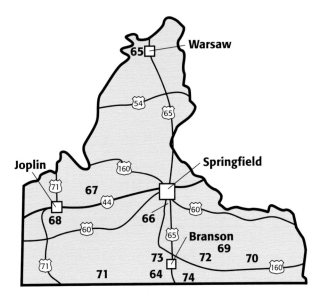

64 Shepherd of the Hills
Fish Hatchery

65 Harry S Truman Reservoir and
Sac-Osage Roadside Park

66 Springfield Conservation
Nature Center

67 Robert E. Talbot
Conservation Area

68 Diamond Grove Prairie Conservation Area and George Washington
Carver National Monument

69 Mark Twain National Forest
Glade Top Trail

70 Caney Mountain Conservation Area

71 Roaring River State Park

72 Mark Twain National Forest
Hercules Glades

73 Ruth and Paul Henning
Conservation Area

74 Drury-Mincy Conservation Area
and Bull Shoals Reservoir

"**O**ur hills ain't high, but our hollers sure are deep." At least that's how early residents of southwest Missouri described their grand hills and hollows. For more than 250 million years, the land surface was exposed to the weather, while the rest of the state was covered by alternating glaciers, seas and floods. Uplifting rock, followed by stream erosion, created the region's winding hollows, steep cliffs and many caves and springs.

Early explorers described the landscape here as a mix of open parklands, glades, savannas and forests. In the region, a glade is an open, rocky meadow with thin, dry soils. A savanna is an open woodland with lush grasses and prairie plants. The grasslands and forests support a great diversity of plants and wildlife.

The White River Hills are dolomite – dramatic and roughly sculpted by the waters of the White River. Large dolomite glades host greater roadrunner, scorpion and tarantula – unusual animals you'd expect to find in the desert Southwest.

64 Shepherd of the Hills Fish Hatchery

In addition to a trout hatchery, Shepherd of the Hills Fish Hatchery offers year 'round wildlife viewing along the upper reaches of Lake Taneycomo. Water from Table Rock Dam is open throughout winter, attracting many species of gulls and waterfowl. Killdeer, belted kingfisher, sandpiper and three species of heron can be seen along Lake Taneycomo.

Wintering birds of prey include black and turkey vultures, osprey and red-shouldered hawk. Watch for mallard, gadwall, bufflehead and wood duck around the hatchery in fall and winter. Hiking trails take you along Lake Taneycomo for scenic views of the land and near feeding areas for shorebirds and aquatic wildlife. Stop by the visitor center to learn more about the trout hatchery and current natural events.

Size: 311 acres   **Nearest town:** Branson

Location: From Branson, travel south on U.S. 65 for 3 miles to the junction of Highway 165. Travel west on 165 for 7 miles (cross Table Rock Dam) to the hatchery entrance.

Contact: Missouri Department of Conservation, P.O. Box 491, Branson, MO 65615, (417) 334-4865

Shepherd of the Hills is one of the best places in Missouri to spot black vultures. They are smaller but more aggressive than turkey vultures.

65 Harry S Truman Reservoir and Sac-Osage Roadside Park

Forest and prairie meet at Truman Reservoir, a sprawling lake filled by the Osage River, South Grand River and Tebo Creek. Below the dam, an overlook provides a view of catfish, paddlefish, gar and other fish swimming near the surface. At the east end of the dam, enjoy a panoramic view of the lake from the visitor center, and hike the .3-mile Kaysinger Bluff Nature Trail.

Early mornings, white-tailed deer and wild turkey feed throughout the area. Watch for osprey and double-crested cormorant. Beaver, red fox, raccoon, coyote, mink and bobcat are best viewed at dusk and dawn. Open woodland savannas brighten with prairie wildflowers in spring and summer. Come winter, bald eagles congregate and roost in large trees. At the Lyndon Q. Skidmore Wetland Management Area (adjoining the reservoir), watch for shorebirds and waterfowl.

Sac-Osage Roadside Park overlooks the junction of the Sac and Osage rivers and Truman Reservoir. Prairie grasses, such as little bluestem and sideoats grama, are found on the rocky glade along with thirteen-lined ground squirrel and fence lizard. Watch for raptors here, especially red-tailed hawk and turkey vulture in spring and Cooper's and sharp-shinned hawks in fall.

Sharp-shinned hawks are 10 to 14 inches long and have short, rounded wings and a long tail.

Size: 166,524 acres   **Nearest town:** Warsaw

Locations: From Highway 7 in Warsaw, travel west 1 mile to the entrance of the dam. Sac-Osage Roadside Park is 3 miles west of Osceola on Highway 82. To access Skidmore Wetland Management Area, drive south of Clinton on Highway 13 for 1 mile to Calvaird Drive. Take Calvaird west for 1.5 miles, cross Business 13, and continue west 1 mile on West Calvaird Drive. Turn north on Hormeyer Street for .5 mile to the entrance on the west.

Contacts for Harry S Truman Reservoir: U.S. Army Corps of Engineers, Route 2, Box 29A, Warsaw, MO 65355, (816) 438-7317; Missouri Department of Conservation, P.O. Box 250, Clinton, MO 64735, (816) 885-6981

Contact for Sac-Osage Roadside Park: Missouri Highway and Transportation Department, Box 14, Osceola, MO 64744, (417) 876-4232

65

66 Springfield Conservation Nature Center

Within the city limits of Springfield, Springfield Conservation Nature Center is an Ozark retreat where visitors can learn about the land and wildlife. And while you're there, you can view wildlife common to the region. The nature center trails cross forests, a restored prairie, a glade, creeks, small marshes and Lake Springfield. A boardwalk goes over the lake's marshy shallows. A total of six trails combine for nearly 3 miles of hiking opportunities.

Year 'round you may see white-tailed deer, raccoons, squirrels, songbirds, turtles, red fox and mink. An indoor wildlife viewing area lets you stop and observe wildlife from inside the facility. Springfield Conservation Nature Center also offers public programs and guided walks to help you learn more about nature in the Ozarks.

Size: 80 acres   **Nearest town:** Springfield

Location: From the intersection of U.S. 65 and U.S. 60 in Springfield, travel 1 mile west on U.S. 60 to the Glenstone exit. Cross over the highway to the frontage road, and follow the signs to the entrance.

Contact: Missouri Department of Conservation, 4600 S. Chrisman, Springfield, MO 65804, (417) 888-4237

Green frogs are usually solitary animals; each deep stream pool may have just one adult living in it. When disturbed, a green frog leaps into the water, often squawking as it jumps.

Squirrels are among the most arboreal of all mammals. Their legs move freely in many directions, and they have claws at the end of flexible, long toes. Their tails help them balance when venturing out on thin, wobbly branches for a nut or flower.

67 Robert E. Talbot Conservation Area

The Spring River twists through the southern edge of this area, attracting herons, ducks, eagles and many other wildlife species. A forest of white and red oaks, elms and maples covers part of Talbot Conservation Area. To see the Spring River's bluffs and wildlife, hike the 1.5-mile trail.

The area is summer habitat for red-shouldered hawks and barn owls. In a group of sycamore trees along the river, a great blue heron rookery is active in spring and summer. Watch for waterfowl, especially mallard ducks, along the river and in nearby fields. You'll see fox and gray squirrels in the bottomlands.

Size: 4,321 acres   **Nearest town:** Joplin

Location: From Joplin, travel east on Interstate 44 for 30 miles to the Stotts City exit. Take Highway 97 north 5 miles to the area entrance. The trailhead is .5 mile down a gravel road past the trail sign.

Contact: Missouri Department of Conservation, 2630 N. Mayfair, Springfield, MO 65803, (417) 895-6880

68 Diamond Grove Prairie Conservation Area and George Washington Carver National Monument

One of the few large prairies of the region, Diamond Grove is a flat grassland with beautiful spring wildflowers. In spring and summer, Indian paintbrush, shooting star, wild indigo, coreopsis, pale purple coneflower and butterfly weed bloom here. Prairie birds to watch for include Henslow's and grasshopper sparrows and upland sandpipers.

Keep an eye out for badger dens, coyotes, short-eared owls and northern harriers. Fritillary and monarch butterflies float among the coneflowers in early summer. An old buffalo wallow is on the prairie, as well as mima mounds – raised spots of uplifted soil where sumac or other unusual plants grow instead of grasses.

While you're in the area, visit George Washington Carver National Monument to see woodland songbirds, frogs, turtles and prairie wildflowers. A visitor center interprets the famous horticulturist's life and offers historical and nature programs. Hike the .75-mile trail through woodland and prairie and past a pond.

Around the pond in spring and summer, you'll see muskrat, fish, frogs and softshell and red-eared slider turtles. Wildflowers on the prairie restoration area are colorful in late summer. During spring and fall migrations, watch for warblers and other songbirds in the forest and trees near the picnic area.

Diamond Grove Prairie Conservation Area

Size: 571 acres **Nearest town:** Joplin

Location: From the junction of Interstate 44 and U.S. 71 in Joplin, take 44 east 9.7 miles to U.S. 71 Alternate. Travel south on 71 Alternate for 6.2 miles, and turn west on County Road V. Travel 3.2 miles on V to Lark Road. Turn north on Lark Road (gravel), and drive 1.3 miles to the parking area.

Contact: Missouri Department of Conservation, 2630 N. Mayfair, Springfield, MO 65803, (417) 895-6880

George Washington Carver National Monument

Size: 210 acres **Nearest town:** Diamond

Location: Travel 1.9 miles west of U.S. 71 Alternate on County Road V, then .7 mile south of V on a Carver road to the entrance on the west side of the road.

Contact: Superintendent, George Washington Carver National Monument, National Park Service, P.O. Box 38, Diamond, MO 64840, (417) 325-4151

69 Mark Twain National Forest Glade Top Trail

To witness the spectacular scenery found in the Ozark's White River Hills, travel Glade Top Trail, a self-guided driving tour of the National Forest Scenic Byways System. Along the way, you'll discover scenic vistas, natural communities, plants, animals and historic sites. The trail pull-offs at Hayden Bald Natural Area, Three Sisters Glades and Caney Lookout Tower all offer beautiful views of the landscape. Greater roadrunners, eastern collared lizards, pygmy rattlesnakes, scorpions and Bachman's sparrows live in the glades and savannas.

While on the trail, watch for grassland songbirds, butterflies, white-tailed deer, wild turkeys, bobwhite quail, squirrels, cottontail rabbits and eastern chipmunks. Flowering dogwood, coneflower, evening primrose and smoke tree add color from spring to fall. When the hardwoods go through October color changes, enjoy the dazzling yellow, orange and red leaf display.

Size: 23 miles

Nearest town: Ava

Location: From the junction of Highway 5 and Highway 14 in Ava, take 5 south 5.1 miles to Highway A. Travel south on A for 3.9 miles to Smallet. Turn south of Smallet on Gravel Road A-409, and travel 3 miles to Forest Road 147 where the trail begins. The trail follows forest roads 147 and 149.

Contact: District Ranger, Mark Twain National Forest, Ava Ranger District, P.O. Box 188, Ava, MO 65608, (417) 683-4428

An adult, male eastern collared lizard will use its bright colors to ward off other males and to attract females in May and June. Adult females are yellowish tan or light brown with faint light spots. Adults range in length from eight to 14 inches.

Broad-winged hawks are best known for their spectacular migrations. Thousands can be seen flying together at one time, in what is referred to as a "kettle of hawks." Broad black and white bands across the tail are a distinguishing feature.

70 Caney Mountain Conservation Area

The natural character of the Ozarks stretches out before you at Caney Mountain. Glades, savannas, forests and small spring-fed creeks cover the rough Caney Hills, providing wonderful wildlife watching opportunities. Caney Mountain hosts a bit of history, too, as the site of Missouri's first wild turkey research project which began under Starker Leopold, Aldo Leopold's son.

At Caney Mountain you'll find rich forests of oak and hickory with clear, cool spring-fed streams full of crayfish and minnows. Caney Mountain Natural Area features open woodland savannas and glades. A trail winds through the natural area, past shady post oak savannas and across stair-stepping rock outcrops of dolomite. Here, shooting star and blue false indigo flower in spring, and purple penstemon, Missouri primrose, blazing star and compass plant bloom in summer.

Listen for Bachman's sparrow, yellow-breasted chat and summer tanager along the trail. Watch for lichen grasshoppers and Texas brush mice as you hike, and look for broad-winged hawks circling above. In late spring, watch for eastern collared lizards basking on sunny glades. Visit Caney Creek in spring to see songbirds, and watch for warblers along the area's trails. Black bears and armadillos sometimes are seen at the area, too. As you travel the main forest road, enjoy the Ozark vistas and look for the state champion black gum tree. Drive this road in late October to view and photograph the colorful leaf display.

Size: 6,694 acres   **Nearest town:** Gainesville

Location: From the junction of Highway 5 and U.S. 160 in Gainesville, travel east on 160 for 1.2 miles to Highway 181. Turn north on 181, and travel 5.7 miles to the area entrance on the west side of the road.

Contact: Missouri Department of Conservation, HCR 3, Box 422, Gainesville, MO 65655, (417) 679-4218

71 Roaring River State Park

A great diversity of Ozark wildlife and rugged, natural land forms keeps visitors returning to Roaring River State Park. Roaring River Spring spews out 20 million gallons of water per day at the foot of a shady bluff. Ferns and mosses cling to the steep ledges above the pool. Roaring River, which has cut a deep valley through the park with clear Ozark spring water, is home to rainbow trout, Ozark sculpin, southern redbelly dace, white and northern hog suckers, longear sunfish, rainbow and orangethroat darters and duskystripe shiner.

Some of the best wildlife viewing is along the river near the campgrounds. Spring through fall, mink and muskrat swim and feed in the river. Raccoon, woodchuck and gray fox are found near the entrance of Pibern Trail. Green and great blue herons are summer residents along the river, and during the winter bald eagles fish the waters.

Cerulean, black-and-white, yellow-throated and other forest warblers move through the trees during spring migration, and sharp-shinned, red-shouldered and broad-winged hawks migrate through the park in fall. Park trails include a hike to the Devil's Kitchen and the 3.5-mile Fire Tower Trail through Roaring River Hills Wild Area.

Fire Tower Trail follows the ridgetops through forest, rocky outcrops and seeping springs to a lookout tower – a chance to see a few rare southwestern animals, such as armadillo and greater roadrunner, along with Ozark species. Watch for woodland wildlife along the trails and search for signs of bobcat and black bear.

Size: 3,358 acres   **Nearest town:** Monett

Location: From Monett, travel Highway 37 south 17 miles to Cassville. Take Highway 112 south of Cassville 7 miles to the park entrance.

Contact: Missouri Department of Natural Resources, Roaring River State Park, Cassville, MO 65625, (800) 334-6946

In the world of mammals, armadillos are unusual because a female always gives birth to four offspring at a time. The quadruplets are identical in every respect, including gender.

72 Mark Twain National Forest
Hercules Glades Wilderness Area

With a visit to Hercules Glades, you'll see a spectacular mosaic of open grasslands, forested knobs, steep glades and narrow valleys. To enjoy the wilderness, hike through the eastern red cedar and oak trees interspersed with prairie grasses of the glades. Redbud, smoke tree and maples lend vibrant color to the landscape in spring and fall, as do Indian paintbrush, penstemon, prairie dock, coneflower, gayfeather and other wildflowers.

While hiking, watch for white-tailed deer, raccoon, cottontail rabbit, wild turkey, bobwhite quail and songbirds. Small lizards and snakes slip among the rocks on the glades, along with an occasional greater roadrunner or tarantula.

Size: 12,315 acres

Nearest town: Branson

Location: From Branson, travel Highway 76 east 14 miles to U.S. 160. Take 160 east 19 miles to Highway 125. Travel north on 125 for 7 miles to the area entrance.

Contact: District Ranger, Mark Twain National Forest, Ava Ranger District, P.O. Box 188, Ava, MO 65608, (417) 683-4428

Scorpions are largely nocturnal and feed on insects and spiders. They are not abundant in Missouri, and here, the sting of a scorpion compares to a wasp or bee. Nevertheless, outdoorspeople should be cautious, especially when exploring rocks or crevices.

In Missouri, the term "glade" refers to rocky openings, usually surrounded by woodlands. They are most common on south- and west-facing slopes where abundant sunshine creates dry conditions.

73 Ruth and Paul Henning Conservation Area

The hills and hollows of Henning Conservation Area provide an oasis for enjoying nature close to the lights of Branson. Dolomite and limestone glades cover dry, rocky slopes, and you'll find plants and animals adapted to the harsh desert-like conditions living here. Little bluestem and Indian grass make tufts of green on the thin glade soils, while smoke tree and Ashe juniper grow slowly, surviving for hundreds of years in deeper soil.

In summer, look for prairie warblers, summer tanagers and white-eyed vireos nesting in the junipers. Common nighthawks nest among the rocks; you can see them zigzag after insects low in the evening sky. Tarantulas and scorpions are common animals of the glade. Fence and eastern collared lizards sun themselves on rocky outcrops along Boulder Glade Trail. This trail crosses open glades and forested hollows within a Designated Natural Area. From the overlook along Boulder Glade Trail, watch for broad-winged hawks.

Dewey Bald Trail winds through a forest to an overlook tower for a scenic view of the surrounding hills and glades. Wildflowers, such as Trelease's larkspur, Indian paintbrush, coneflower, Missouri primrose, gayfeather and prairie dock, cover the glades at Henning in bright colors from early spring through fall.

Size: 1,534 acres   **Nearest town:** Branson

Location: From the junction of U.S. 65 and Highway 248 north of Branson, take 248 west 2.5 miles to the Shepherd of the Hills Expressway. Continue west on the expressway 4 miles to Highway 76. Turn west on 76 for .5 mile to the area entrance on the right.

Contact: Missouri Department of Conservation, 2630 N. Mayfair, Springfield, MO 65803, (417) 895-6880

74 Drury-Mincy Conservation Area and Bull Shoals Reservoir

The White River Hills at Drury-Mincy contributed to the Department of Conservation's deer and turkey restoration, which began in the 1940s. Rich bottomland forests with stands of cane are found along Bee, Fox and Mincy creeks – good places to watch for white-tailed deer and woodland warblers.

Rocky glades and post oak savannas cover south and west hillsides – habitat for tarantula, bluebird, spotted skunk and prairie plants, such as little bluestem, pale purple coneflower, blazing star and larkspur. Watch for armadillo and bobcat late evenings and early mornings. Groups of black and turkey vultures soar above, and Cooper's hawks migrate over the area in spring and fall. To explore the area, hike the short trails that lead off from the roadways.

Nearby, Bull Shoals has scenic bluffs and wetland wildlife to enjoy. At Kissee Mills Park (part of Bull Shoals), there's a walkway and viewing blind overlooking a pond with beaver, mink and muskrat. Spring and fall, watch for migrating waterfowl and shorebirds, gulls and grebes. Nesting colonies of great blue herons are scattered around the lake, as well as egrets, little blue herons and resident belted kingfishers. At dawn and dusk, look for white-tailed deer, wild turkey, red fox and bobcat along the shores. Wintering bald eagles and ospreys fish in the lake.

Bull Shoals Reservoir

Size: 45,440 acres   **Nearest town:** Forsyth

Location: To reach the Kissee Mills portion of Bull Shoals, take Highway 76 east of Forsyth for 2.5 miles to U.S. 160. Travel south on 160 for 1.1 miles to Kissee Mills, then follow the signs 1.6 miles to the park.

Contact: U.S. Army Corps of Engineers, 111 Coy Blvd., Forsyth, MO 65653, (417) 546-4853

Drury-Mincy Conservation Area

Size: 5,699 acres   **Nearest town:** Branson

Location: From the junction of U.S. Business 65 and Highway 76 in Branson, take 76 east 4.5 miles to County Road J. Turn south on J, and continue 5.4 miles to Mincy. At Mincy, continue east on Drury Road to the entrance of the Drury portion. From Mincy, turn south on Gunnison Road .5 mile to the entrance of the Mincy portion.

Contact: Missouri Department of Conservation, 3339 Gunnison Rd., Kirbyville, MO 65679, (314) 334-4830

Ozark Hills

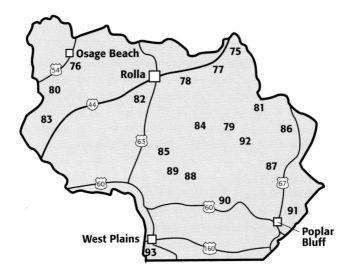

75 Meramec State Park and Meramec Conservation Area
76 Lake of the Ozarks State Park
77 Onondaga Cave State Park
78 Woodson K. Woods Memorial Conservation Area
79 Mark Twain National Forest Bell Mountain Wilderness
80 Ha Ha Tonka State Park
81 Hughes Mountain Natural Area
82 Mark Twain National Forest Lane Spring Recreation Area
83 Bennett Spring State Park
84 Mark Twain National Forest Huzzah Ponds Wildlife Area

85 Montauk State Park
86 Mark Twain National Forest Silver Mines Recreation Area and Mill-stream Gardens Conservation Area
87 Sam A. Baker State Park
88 Ozark National Scenic Riverways – Current and Jacks Fork Rivers
89 Sunklands Conservation Area
90 Peck Ranch Conservation Area
91 Wappapello Reservoir
92 Johnson's Shut-ins and Taum Sauk Mountain State Parks and the Ozark Trail
93 Vanderhoef Memorial State Forest

Traveling through the Ozarks is like going back in time. The forested Missouri mountains look unchanged at first glance. Early visitors to the region marveled at the merging of bluff and prairie, forest and stream, glade and hill.

The hills are ancient and have a diversity of plants and animals unlike any other Missouri region, and perhaps are unrivaled on the continent. Rare habitats host animals and plants found nowhere else in the world. Forests, glades and savannas hide caves, springs, sinkhole ponds and fens. Through erosion, dolomite and sandstone have broken down to create rough and rocky soils not suitable for cultivation.

People of the Ozarks have found livelihood from the rich minerals, forest products and simple subsistence. Short-leaf pine and oak-hickory forests seen by early explorers are gone from our view, but a few of the native pines remain.

75 Meramec State Park and Meramec Conservation Area

To enjoy a scenic Ozark valley surrounded by rich woodlands, visit the Meramec River as it winds past Meramec State Park and Meramec Conservation Area. Hike through the Meramec Upland Forest Natural Area at the state park to see chert woodlands of white and black oaks, hickory and flowering dogwood.

Many miles of trails at both areas take you through forests with glades (or rocky meadows), caves and wet meadows – good viewing for woodland songbirds, wildflowers, and signs of bobcat, black bear and coyote. Fisher Cave at the state park is open seasonally for tours (fee charged). As you walk the cave's mile-long pathway, you'll see pipistrelle and little brown bats.

Watch for river wildlife while canoeing the spring-fed river. You may see great blue and green herons and white-tailed deer along the shore. Watch for mink, muskrat and river otter on the banks, water turtles on logs, and colorful Ozark minnows such as the saddled darter and bleeding shiner in riffles. More than 100 species of fish and many freshwater mussels make this stretch of water one of the richest in Missouri. There is more than 8 miles for you to enjoy, so have your snorkel gear handy. To help you identify some of the fish, stop by the nature center and study the 3,500-gallon aquarium.

Meramec State Park

Size: 6,788 acres   **Nearest town:** Sullivan

Location: Travel Highway 185 south from Sullivan 3 miles. The state park entrance is to the west.

Contact: Missouri Department of Natural Resources, Meramec State Park, 2800 South Highway 185, Sullivan, MO 63080, (800) 334-6946

Meramec Conservation Area

Size: 4,045 acres   **Nearest town:** Sullivan

Location: Travel an additional 1.6 miles past the state park entrance. The conservation area entrance is on the east.

Contact: Missouri Department of Conservation, Meramec Forest District, P.O. Box 248, Sullivan, MO 63080, (314) 468-3335

The soles of ospreys' feet are equipped with spiny, sharp projections that enable the birds to clasp onto slippery prey. Ospreys sometimes are called "fish hawks."

76 Lake of the Ozarks State Park

The state park surrounds the Grand Glaize Arm of Lake of the Ozarks. It is a beautiful mix of Ozark habitats to explore by foot or by boat – forest, stream, glade, savanna, fen, cave and steep bluff. Rising up from the lake, hills covered with oaks and hickories open up to grassy glades. Savannas (grasslands with scattered trees) are another Ozark landscape you'll see as you hike some of the park's nine trails.

While boating, watch for herons and egrets, waterfowl, raccoons, muskrat and mink along the shore and in shallow water. On Squaw's Revenge and Rocky Top trails, view the area from a bluff overlook. Here, watch for vultures and hawks in spring and fall. Rocky Top Trail is a good hike for seeing warblers, vireos, tanagers, wildflowers and flowering dogwoods in April and May.

Coakley Hollow Fen Natural Area is a seepy bog with a boardwalk and self-guiding trail to help you explore unusual plants of the fen and glade (area closed in winter). Along Highway 134 from the stable to the beach road, watch for white-tailed deer, red fox, squirrels, eastern chipmunks, wild turkeys, spring wildflowers and, in fall, vibrant colors of sugar maple. Cave tours are available at Ozark Caverns from March through October. Bats of the cave include big and little browns and eastern pipistrelles.

Size: 17,087 acres   **Nearest town:** Osage Beach

Location: From U.S. 54 at Osage Beach, turn east on Highway 42, and travel 4 miles. Turn south on Highway 134 for .5 mile to the park office.

Contact: Missouri Department of Natural Resources, Lake of the Ozarks State Park, P.O. Box 170, Kaiser, MO 65047, (800) 334-6946; Cave tour information, (314) 346-2500

The eastern pipistrelle is one of 11 species of bats in Missouri. Bats make their homes under tree bark, in caves and barns, and occasionally in the attics of houses. They are not dangerous and, in fact, are highly beneficial because they eat great numbers of night-flying insects pesky to humans.

77 Onondaga Cave State Park

A visit to Onondaga Cave State Park wouldn't be complete without a cave tour, but the forested hills and Meramec River are rich in wildlife too. Onondaga Cave is known for its spectacular cave formations and scenic rooms. Watch for big brown and eastern pipistrelle bats, grotto and slimy salamanders and other cave wildlife. Tours are available March through November (fee charged).

Enjoy scenic bluffs and hills by canoeing the river, where you'll see wildlife such as raccoons, red fox, songbirds, herons, beaver, turtles and fish. Blue Heron Trail takes you past springs, rocky bluffs, glades and an oxbow lake left behind by the river. Spring wildflowers are spectacular along the trail, and summer birds are seen at the lake.

Deer Run Trail goes through forests, glades and to the bluffs overlooking the Meramec. Watch for broad-winged hawks soaring above the valley. In summer, bats are active throughout the park at dusk and dawn. Another impressive geologic feature here is Vilander Bluff Natural Area – a 270-foot cliff rising above the river. Six hundred-year-old eastern red cedars grow atop the bluff.

Size: 1,317 acres   **Nearest town:** Sullivan

Location: Travel Interstate 44 west 12 miles from Sullivan to County Road H. Take H south for 3 miles to the state park entrance.

Contact: Missouri Department of Natural Resources, Onondaga Cave State Park, Route 1, Leasburg, MO 65535, (800) 334-6946

78 Woodson K. Woods Memorial Conservation Area

Whether you're canoeing or just wading at this access to the Meramec River, there's plenty to see. Watch for muskrat, mink, raccoon, wood duck, great blue and green herons, belted kingfisher, Fowler's toad, cricket and green frogs, hellbender salamander, red-eared slider and spiny softshell turtles, northern watersnake, and many aquatic insects near the river. Songbirds, especially warblers, stop in the river valley during spring and fall migration. Fish viewing for smallmouth bass, hogsuckers, long-eared sunfish and darters is spectacular. Nearby, Maramec Spring Park has facilities for camping, trout fishing and picnicking.

Size: 15 acres   **Nearest town:** St. James

Location: Travel 7 miles east of St. James on Highway 8 across the Meramec River to the area entrance.

Contact: Missouri Department of Conservation, P.O. Box 1128 (12655 State Route Y), Rolla, MO 65401, (314) 368-2225

79 Mark Twain National Forest Bell Mountain Wilderness

From vantage points at Bell Mountain, you'll see prairie grasses, wildflowers and scattered shrubs and trees growing on igneous glades of granite. By hiking a trail, you can walk to rocky glades bordered with blackjack oak, winged elm and hickory. Watch for wild turkey, white-tailed deer, cottontail rabbit, coyote and red-tailed hawk. Shut-in Creek – a spring-fed stream – rolls through the valley and attracts songbirds and amphibians. If you're planning a hike, be sure to write for or pick up a trail map before traveling to the area. Trails are not marked, and maps are not available at the trailhead.

Size: 9,027 acres   **Nearest town:** Potosi

Location: From Potosi, take Highway 21 south to Highway 32. Turn west on Highway 32, and travel 7 miles to County Road A. The main trailhead is 5 miles south on County Road A, and the other trailhead is 2 miles off County Road A along Forest Road 2228.

Contact: District Ranger, Mark Twain National Forest, Box 188, Potosi, MO 63664, (314) 438-5427

Barred owls prefer abandoned crow nests or tree cavities for nesting sites. Their "hoohoo-hoohoo" sounds usually occur in a series of eight. Their nickname is "eight-hooter."

80 Ha Ha Tonka State Park

Ha Ha Tonka has an enchanted air, with beautiful rock features and dramatic castle ruins atop a bluff. The karst landscape here is a Designated Natural Area and unmatched in the state: a 250-foot dolomite bluff rising above a chasm, sinkholes, caves, an underground stream, large spring and a natural bridge. It's easy to marvel at the erosive act of water, washing away dolomite, forming caves and then collapsing the great caverns. Nine trails, with a combined distance of more than 7 miles, let you enjoy the scenery and wildlife.

The savannas and rocky meadows or glades are a mixture of woods and prairie. Prairie grasses and wildflowers grow beneath scattered blackjack and post and white oak trees. In spring and summer, yellow coneflower, compass plant, Indian paintbrush, blazing star, sensitive brier, Missouri evening primrose and other wildflowers bloom. The flowers attract many insects, especially butterflies.

While hiking through the savannas – one of which is a Designated Natural Area – watch for eastern bluebird, warbler, pileated woodpecker, screech owl and other birds. The mix of grasslands and trees also is habitat for eastern chipmunks, flying, gray and red fox squirrels, opossums, raccoons, bats and lizards. Along the spring and Niangua Arm of Lake of the Ozarks, turkey vultures and swallows soar overhead, and great blue herons, beaver, muskrat and mink feed and travel. Spring in the forest blooms with Dutchman's breeches, shooting star, columbine, spring beauty, bloodroot and luxuriant ferns.

Size: 2,953 acres   **Nearest town:** Camdenton

Location: From Camdenton, travel west on U.S. 54 for 2 miles. Turn south on County Road D for 2 miles to the state park entrance.

Contact: Missouri Department of Natural Resources, Ha Ha Tonka State Park, Route 1, Box 658, Camdenton, MO 65020, (800) 334-6946

81 Hughes Mountain Natural Area

In a region of extinct volcanoes, Hughes Mountain has igneous glades and forests of oak, hickory and cedar. This and other igneous glades of the St. Francois Mountains have rough, rocky meadows growing little bluestem grass, coreopsis, fame flower, prickly pear cactus, pinweed and rough buttonweed. Lichens and mosses cling to the igneous rocks.

Watch for collared lizards and lichen grasshoppers on the glades and songbirds in the gnarled woods. In late September, a spectacular migration of broad-winged hawks may be seen on cool days after a weather front passes. A trail from the parking lot takes you to the mountain summit for a full view of the countryside.

Size: 330 acres   **Nearest town:** Potosi

Location: From Potosi, travel south on Highway 21 for 11 miles to County Road M. Turn east on M, and travel 4 miles to County Road 541. Turn south on 541 for .3 mile to the area parking lot.

Contact: Missouri Department of Conservation, Box 248, Sullivan, MO 63080, (314) 468-3335

82 Mark Twain National Forest Lane Spring Recreation Area

From trails at Lane Spring, enjoy the woods, glades and vistas along Little Piney Creek. Cedar Bluff Trail (1.5 miles) begins at the picnic ground, climbs the hillside to a dolomite glade, and winds down through the creek bottom. Here, watch for bloodroot, Dutchman's breeches and trillium in spring and bellflower in fall. Insects are plentiful in summer, from dragonflies and other aquatic animals in the stream, to butterflies and katydids in the forests and glades.

Blossom Rock Trail (1-mile loop) located south of the camping area, goes through the creek bottom, past springs and unusual rock formations and through a rocky glade. Near the creek, watch for warblers, wood thrushes, woodpeckers and screech owls.

Size: 397   **Nearest Town:** Rolla

Location: From Rolla, travel south on U.S. 63 for 12 miles to Yancy Mills. The recreation area entrance is on the west side.

Contact: District Ranger, Mark Twain National Forest, 401 Fairgrounds Rd., Rolla, MO 65401, (314) 341-7497

Cedar waxwings almost always travel in flocks and tend to nest in late summer, when small fruits are plentiful for feeding. They are very social and will sometimes pass berries or apple blossoms to one another while sitting in a row together on a branch.

83 Bennett Spring State Park

The gem of this state park is Bennett Spring, a deep, green pool with 100 million gallons of water flowing from it each day. Rainbow trout were introduced to Bennett Spring Branch about 1900 and, from March through October, anglers line the banks to catch trout released from the hatchery. Nearby pools where trout are raised give you a close look at rainbow trout.

Along the banks, you'll find waterfowl, great blue and green herons, killdeer, belted kingfisher and in winter, bald eagle. Mink, beaver, muskrat and river otter are active evenings in the branch and Niangua River. Enjoy the park trails, especially in spring when redbud, oaks, flowering dogwood and woodland wildflowers bloom.

While hiking in wooded areas along the branch, watch for red-tailed and broad-winged hawks, wild turkey, summer tanager, yellow-billed cuckoo, screech, great-horned and barred owls, whip-poor-will, pileated, red-bellied, red-headed and hairy woodpeckers, eastern phoebe, indigo bunting, Carolina chickadee, brown creeper, ruby-crowned kinglet, loggerhead shrike, red-eyed vireo, common yellowthroat, and chipping and field sparrows.

You also may canoe a stretch of the nearby Niangua River. Bennett Spring Hanging Fen Natural Area is a unique natural community along the bluff above Spring Branch.

Size: 3,099 acres   **Nearest town:** Lebanon

Location: From the intersection of Highway 5 and U.S. 64 in Lebanon, travel west on U.S. 64 for 12 miles to the state park entrance.

Contact: Missouri Department of Natural Resources, Bennett Spring State Park, Route 16, Box 750, Lebanon, MO 65536, (800) 334-6946

84 Mark Twain National Forest
Huzzah Ponds Wildlife Area

At Huzzah Ponds you'll find springs, woodlands, streams, ponds and open grasslands all intermingled for interesting nature study. Ponds on the area once were used as a fish hatchery but today attract many kinds of wildlife. Sparrows, warblers, wood thrushes and other songbirds feed and nest at the area spring through fall.

In spring and summer, leopard and green frogs, American and Fowler's toads, salamanders, and red-eared slider, map and spiny soft-shelled turtles are active in the ponds and streams. View raccoons and muskrat year 'round. Travel one of the hiking trails to see spring wildflowers blooming in the woodlands and meadows.

Size: 400 acres   **Nearest town:** Salem

Location: From the junction of Highway 19 and 32 in Salem, travel east on Highway 32 for 16 miles to the parking area on the north.

Contact: District Ranger, Mark Twain National Forest, 1301 S. Main, Salem, MO 65560, (314) 729-6656

Red-headed wood-peckers often inhabit open, agricultural land dotted with dead or dying trees. They gather nuts and acorns and store them in holes and crevices in trees for winter food. Young birds resemble adults, except they have gray heads.

85 Montauk State Park

The Current River comes to life at Montauk State Park. Seven springs create cool waters for trout, and there is a trout hatchery at the park used to stock the river. Trout in the raceways flash their colorful sides as you walk along the pools.

Whether you explore the river valley by trail or while fishing, watch for mink, muskrat, beaver, raccoon and opossum at dawn and dusk. Watch, too, for long-ear sunfish, darters, sculpin and minnows in the river. In winter, bald eagles fish in the river and trout pools. Aquatic insects, including mayflies, caddisflies and dragonflies, are seen best in the early mornings.

Along the river and streams, fire pink and other wildflowers color the banks, and redbud, dogwood and shadbush color the hillsides in spring. Part of the forest is a Designated Natural Area. Canoeing is not allowed at Montauk, but from the Ozark National Scenic Riverways (see page 87) to the south, you can explore by canoe. Wading in the river is permitted for anglers only.

Size: 1,353 acres **Nearest town:** Licking

Location: From the intersection of U.S. 63 and Highway 32 in Licking, take 32 east to Highway 137. Travel 2 miles south on 137 to County Road VV. Turn east on VV for 10 miles to Highway 119, and drive on 119 to the entrance.

Contact: Missouri Department of Natural Resources, Montauk State Park, Route 5, Box 279, Salem, MO 65560, (800) 334-6946

These fleshy, showy bluebells often grow in large groups and will reach two feet in height. They are scattered statewide except for the northwest and southwest.

86 Mark Twain National Forest Silver Mines Recreation Area and Millstream Gardens Conservation Area

Waters of the St. Francis River push their way around granite rocks, through the heart of Millstream Gardens and Silver Mines. Igneous rock carved by the river – areas called shut-ins – are found on both areas. Tiemann Shut-ins, located at the central part of Millstream Gardens, is spectacular. Turkey Creek Trail (2.5 miles) follows the river and connects the two areas. Trails on each side of the river lead to remnants of the area's mining history and interesting rock formations.

Enjoy the flowering dogwoods, redbuds and woodland wildflowers in spring and spectacular colors against the rocky landscape in fall. Watch for wild turkeys, white-tailed deer, lizards, hawks, songbirds, squirrels, raccoons, opossums, mink and eastern chipmunks while visiting both areas. This stretch of river is the only whitewater in Missouri, so kayakers gather here to run the river each spring.

Silver Mines Recreation Area

Size: 600 acres   **Nearest town:** Fredericktown

Location: From Fredericktown, travel west 4 miles on Highway 72 to County Road D. The campground entrance is 3 miles west on D.

Contact: District Ranger, Mark Twain National Forest, Box 188, Potosi, MO 63664, (314) 438-5427

Millstream Gardens Conservation Area

Size: 684 acres   **Nearest town:** Fredericktown

Location: From Fredericktown, follow Highway 72 west for 8.5 miles to the area entrance on the south. Follow the entrance road .5 mile to the parking area and trailhead.

Contact: Missouri Department of Conservation, 2206 W. St. Joseph, Perryville, MO 63775, (314) 547-4537

87 Sam A. Baker State Park

From the summit of Mudlick Mountain down to the shut-ins on Big Creek, Sam A. Baker State Park offers splendid scenery and solitude. The 1.5-mile Shut-ins Trail leads to gorges filled with granite boulders, polished smooth from the swift water. Watch for beaver, raccoons, herons, crayfish and turtles and wintering bald eagles near Big Creek and St. Francis River.

Along the 12-mile Mudlick Trail, hike through Mudlick Mountain Natural Area and Wild Area. The trail winds through oak forests and past deep gorges, shut-ins, glades and bluffs. Enjoy the glades' spring and early summer wildflower bloom and late summer grasses. On the peak of Mudlick Mountain, you'll see trees twisted and gnarled from wind and ice storms.

Watch for white-tailed deer, eastern chipmunks, squirrels, songbirds, wild turkeys, snakes and lizards in the forests and glades. Stop by the visitor center to inquire about viewing hotspots.

Size: 5,168 acres   **Nearest town:** Piedmont

Location: From Piedmont, travel east 11 miles on Highway 34 to Highway 143. Turn north 4 miles on 143 to the park entrance.

Contact: Missouri Department of Natural Resources, Sam A. Baker State Park, Patterson, MO 63956, (800) 334-6946

Other names for the great blue heron include big cranky, long John, poor Joe and Treganza's heron. These birds may have a wingspan up to seven feet and be 42 to 52 inches long. They usually catch fish cross-ways in their bill, then swallow them whole. Sometimes they will spear larger fish.

88 Ozark National Scenic Riverways – Current and Jacks Fork Rivers

As the Current River thunders and rolls through southeast Missouri, it picks up volume from many springs along the way. Floaters enjoy its scenery year 'round. From your canoe, explore unusual habitats and observe animals typical of the Ozark riverways. Enjoy the fish of the river, from bass and sunfish, to suckers and darters. Watch for beaver, muskrat and mink along the banks. Scenic bluffs, beautiful trees and a variety of wildflowers give drama to the course of the river. White-tailed deer and herons walk at the river's edge, and songbirds feed and nest in the trees.

A tributary of the Current, the Jacks Fork River is one of the wildest and most scenic of all Missouri Ozark streams. Clear waters roaring down the valley are surrounded by steep walls and massive cliffs. As you float, allow time for snorkeling and to explore some of the caves along the way. Watch for wood ducks and other waterfowl in the calmer backwaters. In fall, the forests are an array of color.

Size: 134 river miles

Nearest towns: Salem, Van Buren, Mountain View and Eminence

Locations: Salem – travel south on Highway 19 for 19 miles. Turn right on County Road KK. Travel on KK for 6 miles to County Road K. Take K south 1 mile to the campground entrance. Van Buren – take U.S. 60 west and cross the bridge to find a river access. Mountain View – travel 1 mile east to Highway 17. Take 17 north 8 miles to the Buck Hollow entrance. Eminence – an access is located in town, west of the Jacks Fork River bridge on Highway 19.

Contact: National Park Service, Ozark National Scenic Riverways, Box 490, Van Buren, MO 63965, (314) 323-4236

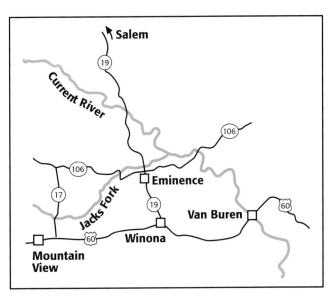

Bobcats usually are active at night, and therefore difficult to see. They hunt mostly at sunrise and sunset, selecting a vantage point to watch for small mammals.

89 Sunklands Conservation Area

An unusual natural area of sinkholes or collapsed caves, Sunklands Conservation Area has an impressive number of sinks as well as rare species of Ozark wildflowers. Sunklands Pond is formed by the collapse of a single cave. The forests are dense, good viewing for songbirds, as well as hawks and owls, wild turkeys, white-tailed deer, fox, bobcats and coyotes. Watch for snakes and other reptiles in the summer.

The area is open year 'round, but due to poor conditions of the roads, a four-wheel drive vehicle is necessary to enter the area. The best way to access the area is by hiking old roads. Before entering Sunklands, be sure to reference a 7.5-minute quadrangle topographic map for Lewis Hollow.

Size: 420 acres   **Nearest town:** Eminence

Location: From Eminence, travel west on Highway 106 for 20 miles to Summersville. Travel north on Highway 17 for 1 mile to County Road K. Turn north on K, and continue for 10 miles. Access to the area is from a logging road west of County Road K-B and east of County Road K.

Contact: Missouri Department of Conservation, Box G, Hwy. 19 N., Eminence, MO 65466, (314) 226-3616

90 Peck Ranch Conservation Area

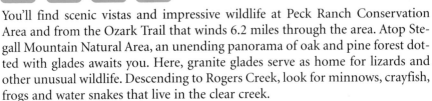

You'll find scenic vistas and impressive wildlife at Peck Ranch Conservation Area and from the Ozark Trail that winds 6.2 miles through the area. Atop Stegall Mountain Natural Area, an unending panorama of oak and pine forest dotted with glades awaits you. Here, granite glades serve as home for lizards and other unusual wildlife. Descending to Rogers Creek, look for minnows, crayfish, frogs and water snakes that live in the clear creek.

A series of beaver ponds near the headquarters is a good place to see beaver at work, wood ducks, and herons and other wading birds. Catching a glimpse of a bobcat or black bear is exciting, and both animals are found in the vast forest habitat. Driving through the area at dusk and dawn, watch for white-tailed deer or wild turkey. In addition, flowering trees and wildflowers are in full bloom from early spring to late summer.

Size: 22,968 acres   **Nearest town:** Winona

Location: From Winona, travel 5 miles east on County Road H to the entrance sign. Turn east and travel 6.5 miles down the gravel entrance road to the area headquarters.

Contact: Missouri Department of Conservation, Box 138, 618 Preacher Roe,West Plains, MO 65775, (417) 256-7161

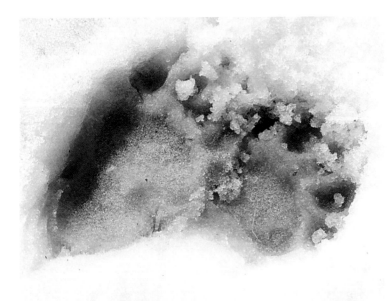

Part of every outdoor experience should include watching for signs left behind by those animals you don't see. For example, watch for broken limbs, signs of foraging or for tracks such as these left by a black bear.

The eastern bluebird is Missouri's state bird. Their musical call – a "tweedle" or "turee" – is unmistakeable.

91 Wappapello Reservoir

Visit Pine Ridge, Lost Creek and Johnson Tract Natural Area trails to enjoy Wappapello Reservoir's wildlife. Pine Ridge Trail, located below the dam, has .5- and .8-mile loops through shortleaf pine and oak and hickory forests. Watch for white-tailed deer, wild turkey, bobwhite quail, cottontail rabbit, wood duck and eastern bluebird.

The trail through Lost Creek Waterfowl Refuge on the northeastern arm of the lake is a 1-mile loop with several stops and an overlook of the refuge. From the trail, watch for ducks and geese during spring and fall migration. In the forest, squirrels, eastern chipmunks, songbirds and spring wildflowers are common. In winter, waterfowl and bald eagles rest and feed in the refuge.

Johnson Natural Area and Trail, located beyond Lost Creek on County Road D, is an area of forest, bluff and glade. If you hike the 5-mile trail in spring, watch for harbinger-of-spring and other wildflowers. Deer and turkey are common throughout the natural area, and view waterfowl and shorebirds around a small wetland. Wappapello's 20-mile section of the Ozark Trail, which begins near the entrance of Sam A. Baker State Park, winds through a pristine area.

Size: 44,351 acres   **Nearest town:** Poplar Bluff

Location: From the intersection of U.S. 60 and 67 in Poplar Bluff, travel east on 60 for 5.5 miles to Highway T. Travel north on T for 11.5 miles to the visitor center on the left.

Contact: U.S. Army Corps of Engineers, HC 2, Box 2349, Wappapello, MO 63966, (314) 222-8562

92 Johnson's Shut-ins and Taum Sauk Mountain State Parks and the Ozark Trail

From the gorges of the Black River at Johnson's Shut-ins up to the peaks at Taum Sauk Mountain, the St. Francois Mountains harbor some of the state's most incredible scenery. Igneous rock exposed in the region was formed more than a billion years ago, but the rhyolite and granite defy their age with beauty. At Johnson's Shut-ins, walk the trail to the shut-ins and deep gorge. Shut-ins Trail, a 2.5-mile loop, crosses a rocky slope of oak and pine forest with scenic overlooks of the gorge along the way. In spring and summer, ferns and wildflowers color the glades and forest.

Taum Sauk Section of the Ozark Trail takes off from Johnson's Shut-ins to Proffit Mountain, Mina Sauk Falls and Taum Sauk Mountain – the highest point in the state at 1,772 feet above sea level. The region is noted for its diverse plants – more than 900 species, including witch hazel, sundrop, fire pink and many orchids. Watch for songbirds, hawks and lizards as you hike. Fall is a spectacular time to visit Taum Sauk and absorb the colors of autumn.

Johnson's Shut-ins State Park

Size: 7,849 acres   **Nearest town:** Lesterville

Location: From Lesterville, travel west on Highway 72 for 3 miles to County Road N. Turn north on N for 7 miles to the park entrance.

Contact: Missouri Department of Natural Resources, Johnson's Shut-ins State Park, HCR 1, Box 126, Middlebrook, MO 63656, (800) 334-6946

Taum Sauk Mountain State Park

Size: 6,508 acres   **Nearest town:** Ironton

Location: Travel south on Highway 21 for 5 miles to County Road CC. Follow CC west for 3 miles to the park entrance.

Contact: Missouri Department of Natural Resources, Taum Sauk Mountain State Park, HCR 1, Box 126, Middlebrook, MO 63656, (800) 334-6946. For information about the Ozark Trail, contact the Ozark Trail Coordinator, Missouri Department of Natural Resources, Division of Parks and Historic Preservation, P.O. Box 176, Jefferson City, MO 65102

Cardinal flowers grow in wet places, such as streamsides, ponds and sloughs, in south and central Missouri.

93 Vanderhoef Memorial State Forest

At Vanderhoef, enjoy a woodland hike and overlook of Spring River. The area trail loops .8 mile through the forested hills. Watch for woodland songbirds as you hike, and enjoy the wildflowers and trees blooming in spring and early summer. The trail takes you along the banks of Spring River and to an overlook. Here, view beaver and muskrat, herons, frogs, turtles, fish and crayfish.

Size: 140 acres   **Nearest town:** West Plains

Location: From the intersection of U.S. 63 and 160 in West Plains, travel south on 160 for 3 miles to County Road JJ. Turn south on JJ for 7 miles to County Road 962. Take 962 southeast for .5 mile to County Road 811. Turn south on 811 for .4 mile to the area entrance on the east.

Contact: Missouri Department of Conservation, P.O. Box 138, 618 Preacher Roe, West Plains, MO 65775, (417) 256-7161

Bootheel

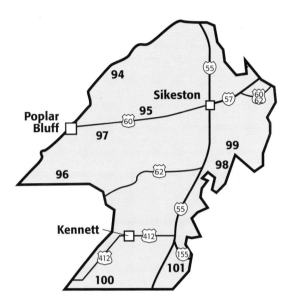

94 Mingo National Wildlife Refuge
and Duck Creek Conservation Area
95 Holly Ridge Conservation Area
96 Allred Lake Natural Area
97 Otter Slough Conservation Area
98 Donaldson Point Conservation Area

99 Big Oak Tree State Park
100 Hornersville Swamp
Conservation Area
101 Caruthersville Rookery
Conservation Area

A short 100 years ago, the Bootheel was a bald cypress and tupelo gum swampland with forested areas. At one time the Mississippi River meandered through much of the area, and when it shifted east about 18,000 years ago, it left behind rich soils. In some places the soils are hundreds of feet thick. The lowland was a basin for silt, serving as the upper portion of the Gulf of Mexico several hundred thousand years ago. Within the fertile soils, trees quickly grew to enormous sizes, and a few of these giants still stand.

To open the rich soils for agriculture, ditches were constructed to drain the swamps, and trees were cleared in the early 1900s. Today, remaining swamps and bottomland forests are habitat for species such as banded pygmy sunfish and swamp rabbit.

Crowley's Ridge, a chain of hills along the northern and western parts of the Bootheel, is the only remaining upland of the region. The hills were carved by the Mississippi and Ohio rivers, swollen with glacial meltwaters. Springs, seeps and the fertile soils form unusual natural communities, home to rare plants such as American beech, ferns and orchids.

94 Mingo National Wildlife Refuge and Duck Creek Conservation Area

Together, Mingo and Duck Creek are more than 27,000 acres of bottomland forest and cypress swamp, habitat with rich soils, towering trees, abundant water and diverse wildlife. Mingo has three hiking trails, including the 1-mile Boardwalk Nature Trail to Rockhouse Cypress Marsh. While walking the trail, watch for squirrels, muskrat, beaver, pileated woodpeckers, warblers, wood ducks, gray and green treefrogs, turtles and water snakes. From observation towers on Boardwalk, Bluff Road, Red Mill Drive and Monopoly Lake, you get a panoramic view of the marsh.

November to March, watch for Canada and snow geese, tundra and trumpeter swans, bald eagle and mallard, pintail and gadwall ducks. On Sundays in April, October and November, the 25-mile auto tour route is open. Watch for white-tailed deer, wild turkey, raccoon, barred owl and red-shouldered hawk during the two-hour drive. At Duck Creek, visit Pool 1 to view waterfowl from October through March and bald eagles year 'round. Watch for river otter, heron, pie-billed grebe and mink. Pool fish include unusual species such as chain pickerel, flier and bowfin.

Mingo National Wildlife Refuge

Size: 21,676 acres   **Nearest town:** Poplar Bluff

Location: From U.S. 60 in Poplar Bluff, travel east 14 miles to Highway 51. Take 51 north at Fisk, and drive 13.5 miles. The entrance to the area is 1 mile north of Puxico on the west side.

Contact: Mingo National Wildlife Refuge, Route 1, Box 103, Puxico, MO 63960, (314) 222-3589.

Duck Creek Conservation Area

Size: 6,190 acres   **Nearest town:** Poplar Bluff

Location: From U.S. 60 in Poplar Bluff, travel east 14 miles to Highway 51. Take 51 north at Fisk and drive 19.5 miles. The entrance is on the west side of the road.

Contact: Missouri Department of Conservation, Route 1, Box 186, Puxico, MO 63960, (314) 222-3247

Early morning is the best time to see wood ducks as they fly from roost sites to forest areas. Their preferred food is acorns.

95 Holly Ridge Conservation Area

Holly Ridge is located on Crowley's Ridge, a landscape of sand and gravel that was deposited millions of years ago at the edge of an ancient sea. The area is covered with oak and hickory trees, good viewing for woodland songbirds, white-tailed deer, wild turkeys and wildflowers.

Beech Springs and Holly Ridge natural areas have rare and unusual plants, such as American holly and farkleberry. At Beech Springs, you'll find a natural pond on a hillside surrounded by large oak trees. The seep is rich in plants, especially alder, spicebush, sedges, ferns, mosses and orchids. Other unusual features of Holly Ridge include a forest of tulip, beech and alder trees and spring-fed streams with rare animals.

Size: 1,000 acres   **Nearest town:** Dexter

Location: From Dexter, take U.S. 60 east 2 miles to County Road 531. Take 531 north .7 mile to County Road N. Turn left on N for .5 mile to a gravel road on the right. Turn on the gravel road, and travel north 1.1 miles to the parking area.

Contact: Missouri Department of Conservation, 1207 N. One Mile Rd., Dexter, MO 63841, (314) 624-7483

Designated natural areas, such as Allred Lake, are the best examples of each remaining terrestial and aquatic community type within each region of the state. Several are included in this guide.

96 Allred Lake Natural Area

Allred Lake is an ancient and majestic swamp with bald cypress trees more than 500 years old. From the viewing deck, take time to enjoy the cypress and tupelo gum reflecting on the stained waters. Water hickory, water locust, water and Nuttal's oaks, swamp cottonwood and sweetgum are trees of the swamps and forests.

The lake has rare fish, such as the tailight shiner and swamp darter, but you're most likely to see bowfin and gar. Watch for aquatic salamanders such as amphiumas and sirens, along with green treefrogs, leopard frogs, turtles and water snakes. In summer, be prepared to find mosquitoes (repellent is recommended), crickets, katydids and butterflies.

Size: 160 acres   **Nearest town:** Poplar Bluff

Location: From Poplar Bluff, take Highway 53 south 1 mile. Turn right on Highway 142, and travel 13 miles. At the intersection of 142 and County Road HH, turn east on HH and then south on H. Travel H for 3 miles until the paved road turns to gravel. The entrance is to the south.

Contact: Missouri Department of Conservation, 1207 N. One Mile Rd., Dexter, MO 63841, (314) 624-7483

97 Otter Slough Conservation Area

Otter Slough is a scenic mix of cypress swamp and river slough visited by thousands of waterfowl each year – and home to a few river otters. Wintering migratory waterfowl are the most abundant wildlife December through February, with thousands of ducks and an average of 100,000 snow geese. In early March through mid-May, shorebirds such as yellowlegs, black-bellied plover, pectoral sandpiper and black-necked stilt come to areas of shallow water to feed.

In summer, watch for water mammals, frogs, turtles and snakes. Walk a 1-mile nature trail near the headquarters, and watch for warblers, woodpeckers and other songbirds. Take a .5-mile hike to the north end of Otter Slough to visit Bradyville Natural Area – a bottomland forest and swamp of overcup and post oak, tupelo and cypress trees.

Size: 4,863 acres   **Nearest town:** Dexter

Location: Take U.S. 60 west from Dexter 1 mile to County Road ZZ. Travel south on ZZ for 9 miles to the area entrance at County Road 675. Follow 675 for 2.5 miles to the headquarters at Otter Lake.

Contact: Missouri Department of Conservation, Route 3, Box 307, Dexter, MO 63841, (314) 624-5821

98 Donaldson Point Conservation Area

Inside a big loop of the Mississippi River, Donaldson Point Conservation Area has river on two sides and a forest of cottonwood, sycamore and maple in the middle. Bald cypress trees are found in the sloughs, and oak and walnut grow on higher ground. Watch for Mississippi kites flying above treetops, songbirds in the woodlands, and killdeer, the endangered least tern and other shorebirds along the river. In the ponds and sloughs, view beaver, muskrat, mink and other water mammals.

Size: 5,785 acres   **Nearest town:** New Madrid

Location: Take County Road U east out of New Madrid for 1 mile to County Road WW. Travel on WW east for 3.2 miles to County Road AB. Take AB for 4 miles to the area entrance.

Contact: Missouri Department of Conservation, Box 131, New Madrid, MO 63869, (314) 748-5134

Big Oak Tree State Park is home to this champion bur oak (left). Throughout most of the state, deer (below) once again are common after falling to extremely low numbers in the 1930s. White-tailed deer fawns begin to follow their mothers and eat solid food when they are three to eight weeks old. Fawns stay with their mothers until they are six to eight months old and capable of having young of their own.

99 Big Oak Tree State Park

To experience the Bootheel's giant swamplands as early explorers once did, visit Big Oak Tree State Park. The park appears on the horizon as an island of forest growing on fertile earth. You'll be amazed by the size of the trees and wealth of wildlife. Within the park, swamp rabbits are common in the shrubby swamp, while bald cypress, swamp chestnut, sycamore and bur oak are trees of the swamp.

Walk the boardwalk trail through Big Oak Tree Natural Area to see many of Missouri's largest trees – nine state champions – as well as raccoons, squirrels, songbirds, water and black snakes and turtles. And in summer, the mosquitoes will find you, so come prepared with repellent. Herons and egrets stalk minnows and crayfish in the shallow waters, and barred owls, yellow-billed cuckoos, wood thrushes, hooded and prothonotary warblers, Mississippi kites and wood ducks are common in summer.

Size: 1,007 acres

Nearest town: Sikeston

Location: From the junction of Interstate 55 and U.S. 60, take 55 south 8 miles to Highway 80. Travel east 11 miles to Highway 102. Turn south on 102 and travel 12 miles to the park entrance.

Contact: Missouri Department of Natural Resources, Big Oak Tree State Park, Route 2, Box 343, East Prairie, MO 63845, (800) 334-6946

Green treefrogs prefer to live near permanent bodies of water such as cattail marshes, cypress swamps or river sloughs. They live in southeastern Missouri.

100 Hornersville Swamp Conservation Area

A swampy forest of overcup oak, green ash and bald cypress trees, Hornersville Swamp is a small remnant of the 2.4 million acres of bottomland forest that once covered the Bootheel. The swamp's plants and animals are diverse, and the habitat supports beaver, river otters, swamp rabbits, mink, muskrat, raccoons, songbirds, wading birds, waterfowl, frogs, salamanders, turtles and snakes. In winter, view thousands of mallard and wood ducks on the area. Watch for white-tailed deer, squirrels, cottontail rabbits and wild turkeys in the uplands.

Size: 3,381 acres   **Nearest town:** Hornersville

Location: In Hornersville, turn east on Pecan Street, and follow the sign to Hornersville Access. Travel 2 blocks on Pecan Street, and turn left by the access sign. Follow the road to the boat access and parking area. To access the area by foot, take Highway 164 north from Hornersville. Follow 164 east to County Road TT. Go south on TT for 7 miles to the Arkansas state line. Turn west on the gravel road 3.2 miles to access the east side of the area.

Contact: Missouri Department of Conservation, Route 3, Box 307, Dexter, MO 63841, (314) 624-5821

101 Caruthersville Rookery Conservation Area

Caruthersville Rookery, a small area of willows and open water, hosts thousands of nesting herons and egrets each summer. Visit the area from May to July, and watch quietly from the parking lot along the west side. Birds of the nesting colony include great egrets and little blue herons. Watch, too, for cattle egrets, great blue herons, yellow-crowned and black-crowned night herons, snowy egrets and, occasionally, anhingas. The site has hosted as many as 2,500 nests, so use binoculars to observe the nests and handsome chicks.

Size: 43 acres   **Nearest town:** Caruthersville

Location: From Caruthersville, take Interstate 155 south to County Road Y. Travel south on Y for .5 mile and turn west. Continue west 1 mile, and turn north .8 mile to the parking lot on the east side of the road.

Contact: Missouri Department of Conservation, 1207 N. One Mile Rd., Dexter, MO 63841, (314) 624-7483

Little blue herons (left) grow to be 25 to 30 inches tall. They are generally silent, but occasionally let out low clucking or croaking sounds. They prefer ponds, lakes, marshes, meadows and marshy shores of streams. Sometimes they can be seen following a plow picking through overturned soil for insect larvae. Cattle egrets (right) are common in Missouri but not native to the state. They originated in Africa, spread to South America in the early 1900s and began nesting in Florida in the '40s. Their range continues to expand.

Cooperating Land Management Agencies

 Missouri Department of Conservation – owns and manages more than 900,000 acres at 940 Conservation Areas and many facilities, including nature centers, regional service centers and visitor centers. Its mission is to manage the state's forests, fisheries and wildlife. Missouri Department of Conservation, P.O. Box 180, Jefferson City, MO 65102, (314) 751-4115

 Missouri Department of Natural Resources – administers 79 state parks and historic sites, comprising approximately 130,000 acres. The state park system's mission is to preserve and interpret the state's most outstanding natural features and cultural landmarks while providing recreational opportunities. Missouri Department of Natural Resources, P.O. Box 176, Jefferson City, MO 65102, (800) 334-6946

 St. Louis County Parks Department – manages 66 county parks totaling more than 11,000 acres for recreation and wise use of natural resources. St. Louis County Parks, 41 S. Central Ave., Clayton, MO 63105, (314) 889-2863

 U.S. Fish and Wildlife Service – administers more than 60,000 acres of wildlife habitat in Missouri, including seven wildlife refuges and a national fish hatchery. Its mission is to conserve, protect and enhance the nation's fish and wildlife and their habitats for the benefit of the American people. Major responsibilities include migratory birds, endangered species and interjurisdictional fisheries management. U.S. Fish and Wildlife Service, Bishop Henry Whipple Federal Building, Fort Snelling, MN 55111, (612) 725-3507, or refer to contact information for national wildlife refuge viewing sites.

USDA Forest Service – manages 1.5 million acres of wildlife habitat in south and central Missouri as the Mark Twain National Forest. Its mandate is to protect, improve and wisely use the natural resources for multiple purposes, including recreation, wilderness, timber, fish and wildlife. Mark Twain National Forest, U.S. Forest Service, 401 Fairgrounds Rd., Rolla, MO 65401, (314) 341-7497

 University of Missouri – maintains Tucker Prairie to preserve native grasslands and provide a location for ecological research. University of Missouri, Division of Biological Sciences, 110 Tucker Hall, Columbia MO 65211, (314) 882-6659

Jackson County Parks and Recreation Department
– administers county parklands for recreation and wildlife habitat. Jackson County Parks and Recreation, 22807 Woods Chapel Rd., Blue Springs, MO 64015, (816) 795-8200

National Park Service – keeps more than 134 miles of clear, spring-fed streams accessible in southern Missouri and operates George Washington Carver National Monument, Wilson's Creek National Battlefield, and Jefferson National Expansion Memorial, Harry S Truman and Ulysses S. Grant national historic sites in the state. Its mission is to conserve scenery, natural and historical objects, and wildlife and provide for the enjoyment of present and future generations. National Park Service, U.S. Department of the Interior, Ozark National Scenic Riverways, Box 490, Van Buren, MO 63965, (314) 323-4236; George Washington Carver National Monument, P.O. Box 38, Diamond, MO 64840, (417) 325-4151

Martha Lafite Thompson Nature Sanctuary – manages 100 acres privately for wildlife habitat and nature study. Martha Lafite Thompson Nature Sanctuary, 407 N. LaFrenz, Liberty, MO 64068, (816) 781-8598

Ellisville Parks and Recreation Department – manages parks and recreation facilities for the community. Ellisville Parks and Recreation, 16 Keifer Creek Rd., Ellisville, MO 63011, (314) 227-7371

U.S. Army Corps of Engineers – is the steward of the land and water at Corps water resources projects. Its mission is to manage and conserve those natural resources consistent with ecosystem management principles, while providing quality public outdoor recreation experiences. It manages 10 major lakes in Missouri along with the Mississippi riverway. The Corps also is responsible for several wildlife mitigation projects on the Missouri River and promotes watchable wildlife and enjoyment of natural resources on all Corps lands. U.S. Army Corps of Engineers, St. Louis District, 1222 Spruce St., St. Louis, MO 63101, (314) 331-8622; Kansas City District, 716 Federal Building, 601 E. 12th St., Kansas City, MO 64106, (816) 426-6816

City of Gladstone – manages parks for public enjoyment and recreation, along with natural resource conservation. City of Gladstone, 7010 N. Holmes, Gladstone, MO 64118, (314) 436-2200

Finding Field Guides

Field guides are available at bookstores or specialty nature stores. Be sure to thumb through several different kinds to find ones that suit you and your level of expertise. Here are some suggested titles.

Amphibians and reptiles

Amphibians and Reptiles of Missouri. Tom R. Johnson. Missouri Department of Conservation, 1987.

A Field Guide to Reptiles and Amphibians: Eastern and Central North America. Roger Conant and Joseph Collins. Peterson Field Guide Series. Boston: Houghton Mifflin, 1991.

Birds

The Birder's Handbook: A Field Guide to the Natural History of North American Birds. Paul R. Ehrlich, David S. Dobkin and Darryl Wheye. New York: Simon and Schuster, 1988.

Birds of North America. Chandler S. Robbins, et al. Golden Field Guide Series. Golden Press, 1983.

A Field Guide to Eastern Birds: A Field Guide to Birds East of the Rockies. Roger Tory Peterson. Peterson Field Guide Series. Boston: Houghton Mifflin, 1984.

Field Guide to the Birds of North America. Shirley L. Scott. 2nd ed. Washington, D.C.: National Geographic Society, 1983.

A Guide to the Birding Areas of Missouri. Kay Palmer. Audubon Society of Missouri, 1993.

Crayfish

An Introduction to the Crayfish of Missouri. Free brochure by the Missouri Department of Conservation.

Fish

Fishes of Missouri. William L. Pflieger. Missouri Department of Conservation, 1975.

Fishes of the Central United States. Joseph R. Tomelleri and Mark E. Eberle. Lawrence: University Press of Kansas, 1990.

Insects

Butterflies and Moths of Missouri. Richard Heitzman and Joan Heitzman. Missouri Department of Conservation, 1987.

A Field Guide to the Butterflies of North America, East of the Great Plains. Peterson Field Guide Series. Boston: Houghton Mifflin, 1951.

A Field Guide to the Insects of America North of Mexico. Donald J. Borror and Richard E. White. Peterson Field Guide Series. Boston: Houghton Mifflin, 1970.

Simon and Schuster's Guide to Insects. Ross H. Arnett, Jr. and Richard L. Jaques, Jr. New York: Simon and Schuster, 1981.

Mammals

A Field Guide to Animal Tracks. Olaus Murie. 2nd ed. Peterson Field Guide Series. Boston: Houghton Mifflin, 1975.

A Field Guide to the Mammals. William H. Burt. 3rd ed. Peterson Field Guide Series. Boston: Houghton Mifflin, 1976.

The Wild Mammals of Missouri. Charles W. Schwartz and Elizabeth R. Schwartz. Columbia: University of Missouri Press, 1981.

Maps

Missouri Hiking Trails. Raymond Gass. Missouri Department of Conservation, 1990.

Missouri Ozark Waterways. Oz Hawksley. Missouri Department of Conservation, 1989.

Missouri's Conservation Atlas – A Guide to Exploring Your Conservation Lands. Missouri Department of Conservation, 1995.

U.S. Geological Survey Maps. U.S. Department of the Interior, Distribution Branch, Box 25286, Federal Center, Denver, CO 80225

Mollusks

Missouri Naiades. Ronald D. Oesch. Missouri Department of Conservation, 1984.

Plants

Field Guide to Missouri Ferns. James S. Key. Missouri Department of Conservation, 1982.

A Field Guide to Trees of the Eastern United Sates and Canada. George A. Petrides. Peterson Field Guide Series. Boston: Houghton Mifflin, 1988.

A Field Guide to Wildflowers of Northeastern and North Central North America. Roger Tory Peterson and Margaret McKenney. Peterson Field Guide Series. New York: Houghton Mifflin, 1968.

Flora of Missouri. Julian A. Steyermark. Ames: University of Iowa Press, 1964.

A Key to Missouri Trees in Winter. Jerry Cliburn and Ginny Wallace. Missouri Department of Conservation, 1992.

Missouri Wildflowers. Edgar Denison. Missouri Department of Conservation, 1989.

Trees of North America. C. Frank Brockman. New York: Golden Press, 1986.

Missouri's 12 Hotspots

August A. Busch Memorial (#36) and
Marais Temps Clair Conservation Areas (#30)
In the fields and woodlands at Busch, watch for deer, small mammals and songbirds. The ponds attract waterfowl, shorebirds and wading birds. Marias Temps Clair has marsh birds, turtles, frogs, snakes, hawks, geese and ducks to watch in summer, and waterfowl and shorebird migrations in spring and fall.

Fountain Grove Conservation Area and
Swan Lake National Wildlife Refuge (#9)
Spring and fall migration are excellent viewing times at Fountain Grove and Swan Lake, when the ducks, geese, shorebirds and pelicans come through. Bald eagles spend fall and winter on the areas. Watch for wetland wildlife such as river otters and muskrat year 'round and, in summer, songbird watching is a favorite activity.

Ruth and Paul Henning Conservation Area (#73) and
Shepherd of the Hills Fish Hatchery (#64)
Spring on the glades at Henning means showy wildflowers, nesting songbirds and basking lizards. Enjoy the rolling hills from the overlooks, too. The fish hatchery is a fascinating place to see trout, but watch for wintering vultures and waterfowl, herons, shorebirds and songbirds as well.

Lake of the Ozarks State Park (#76)
The scenic hills are home to songbirds, hawks, vultures, red fox, deer, wild turkeys and wildflowers, while the water's edge is inhabited by herons, raccoons, mink and waterfowl. Visit Ozark Caverns (March-October) to see bats and other cave animals.

Mingo National Wildlife Refuge and
Duck Creek Conservation Area (#94)
The cypress swamps are excellent viewing for bald eagles, including several nests on the areas. Many warblers and other songbirds are seen in spring and summer, along with turtles, river otters, deer, wild turkeys, fish and hawks. The wintering snow geese, ducks and trumpeter swans are spectacular.

Ozark National Scenic Riverways –
Current and Jacks Fork Rivers (#88)
Steep bluffs are a nice backdrop for the plants and animals of the spring-fed riverways. Fish and crayfish move beneath your canoe, herons and kingfishers hunt nearby, and turtles and snakes bask on logs. Songbirds move through the trees, and ferns and wildflowers grow on the banks and bluffs.

Prairie State Park (#54)
Experience the tallgrass prairie's wildlife and wildflowers at Prairie State Park. Herds of bison and elk roam the scenic grasslands. Spring activities include the courtship of prairie chickens, nesting songbirds and Indian paintbrush in flower, followed by the coneflowers, butterflies and reptiles of summer.

Schell-Osage Conservation Area (#50)

Waterfowl, pelicans and shorebirds at Schell-Osage are best viewed in spring and fall. All seasons, watch for wild turkeys, river otters and deer, and see herons, turtles and songbirds in summer. Wintering bald eagles are popular viewing, too.

Ted Shanks Conservation Area (#22)

Alive with the wildlife of the big river, Shanks plays host to the migrations of shorebirds, ducks and geese in spring and fall. Summer brings herons and egrets from a nearby nest colony, songbirds, hawks and marsh birds. Watch for muskrat and other water mammals year 'round.

Squaw Creek National Wildlife Refuge (#5)

For year 'round wildlife viewing, Squaw Creek is one of the best locations in the state. During fall migration, snow geese, ducks, hawks and bald eagles are astounding, while spring brings shorebirds and marsh birds. Other times of the year you'll see waterfowl as well as deer, raccoons, beaver, muskrat, coyotes and many animals of the prairie marsh.

Organizations and Facilities

Here are some of the state's conservation organizations and additional facilities. Contact them about exhibits, field trips, programs and for additional information about nature viewing opportunities in Missouri.

Cape Girardeau Regional Service Center, Missouri Department of Conservation, 2302 County Park Dr., Cape Girardeau, MO 63701, (314) 290-5730

Conservation Federation of Missouri, 728 W. Main St., Jefferson City, MO 65101, (314) 634-2322

Missouri Audubon Council, 619 Norris Dr., Jefferson City, MO 65109

Missouri Native Plant Society, P.O. Box 20073, St. Louis, MO 63144-0073

Missouri Prairie Foundation, P.O. Box 200, Columbia, MO 65205

Rockwoods Reservation, Missouri Department of Conservation, 2751 Glencoe Rd., Glencoe, MO 63038

Sierra Club, Ozark Chapter, P.O. Box 364, Jefferson City, MO 65102

St. Joseph Regional Service Center, Missouri Department of Conservation, 701 N. E. College Dr., St. Joseph, MO 64507, (816) 271-3100

St. Louis Zoo, Forest Park, St. Louis, MO 63110, (314) 781-0900

Top 25 Species

Listed below are some of the popular species, outstanding locations and best seasons to view Missouri wildlife. Refer to individual site descriptions for more information about the plants or animals.

Species	Spring	Summer	Fall	Winter
Bald eagle	91, 94	94	5, 9, 42, 94	5, 9, 21, 23, 24 25, 31, 42, 50, 65, 91, 94
Bats	75, 76, 77	32, 75, 76, 77	32, 75, 76, 77	
Beaver	31, 74, 83, 88, 90	9, 31, 74, 83, 88, 90	5, 9, 74, 83, 88, 90	31, 88
Butterflies	46, 69	15, 31, 46, 51, 54, 58, 68, 69	15, 46	
Collared lizard	58, 69, 70, 73, 81	58, 61, 63, 69, 73 81	63, 69, 73	
Crayfish	26, 40, 75, 88	40, 48, 70, 75, 87, 88	26, 70, 75, 87, 88	75
Ferns	71, 88, 92	60, 61, 71, 88, 92	60, 61, 71, 88	
Flowering dogwood	26, 27, 34, 37, 41 69, 72, 75, 76, 83, 86		42, 69, 72, 76	
Great blue heron	12, 30, 36, 49, 67, 74, 76, 88, 101	1, 12, 14, 20, 36, 49, 50, 67, 74, 76, 88, 101	49, 74, 76, 78, 88	
Greater prairie chicken	46, 48, 51, 52, 53, 54	46, 48	52	52
Mink	63, 75, 78, 88, 98	56, 63, 75, 78, 88	63, 75, 88, 98	56, 75, 78, 88
Muskrat	9, 71, 74, 75, 78, 80, 88	31, 45, 71, 74, 75, 78, 80, 88	9, 31, 45, 71, 74, 78, 88	9, 88, 100
Orchids		10, 28, 60, 92		
Osprey			9, 22, 42, 64, 65	22, 24, 42, 64, 65, 74, 76
Rainbow trout	71, 64, 83, 85	71, 64, 83, 85	71, 64, 83, 85	71, 64, 83, 85
Redbud tree	27, 37, 42, 72, 83, 86		27, 72	
River otter	5, 9, 39, 50, 65, 94, 97	9, 39, 65, 94, 97, 100	9, 65, 94, 97	9, 39, 50, 65, 94, 97, 100
Ruffed grouse	11, 27, 34, 75		75	11
Snow geese	5, 23, 50, 97		5, 23, 50, 57, 97	5, 13, 57, 97
Sugar maple			34, 35, 37, 41, 42, 43, 76, 80, 88	
Stream fish	39, 75, 78	39, 71, 75, 85, 88	71, 75, 85, 88	75, 85, 88
Turkey vulture	35, 43, 65, 74, 76	21, 76	4, 43, 64, 74	64
White pelican	9, 50		9, 50	
White-tailed deer	5, 45, 65, 74, 78, 88, 90	5, 32, 63, 69, 74 88	5, 32, 36, 44, 63, 65, 69, 74, 78, 88	5, 36, 45, 65, 74, 78, 90
Wild turkey	39, 46, 65, 69, 70, 74	39, 65, 70, 74, 90	39, 46, 69, 70, 74, 86, 90	39, 50, 65, 70, 74

Area Index (with page numbers)